MEETING CHRIST IN SCRIPTURE

MEETING CHRIST IN SCRIPTURE

DIANNE AND ROGER MILLER

ST. PATRICK'S SEMINARY LIBRARY
MENLO PARK, CALIFORNIA
94025

Paulist Press, New York, N.Y., Ramsey, N.J.

Copyright © 1979 by
Roger and Diane Miller

Library of Congress
Catalogue Card Number: 79-90005

ISBN: 0-8091-2251-0

Published by
Paulist Press

Editorial Office:
1865 Broadway
New York, N.Y. 10023

Business Office:
545 Island Road
Ramsey, N.J. 07446

Printed and bound in the
United States of America

CONTENTS

CHAPTER 1
Meeting Christ in Scripture   8

CHAPTER 2
Study, Share and Pray Scripture   9

CHAPTER 3
Home Scripture Programs   22

CHAPTER 4
Parish Scripture Programs   51

CHAPTER 5
Youth Ministry Scripture Programs   97

CHAPTER 6
Scripture Study and Prayer Resources   116

ACKNOWLEDGEMENTS

We wish to thank the many authors and speakers whose writings and presentations on Scripture have enlightened and inspired us in recent years. Their material has made Scripture Programs possible and within the reach of every parishioner. Our gratitude to the Los Angeles Archdiocesan Adult Religious Education Office and the Southern California (Charismatic) Renewal Center who have co-sponsored the coordination and presentation of the Scripture Programs in the Los Angeles Archdiocese.

Many people have made this book possible. By their love, personal sharings and support they have "coauthored" the many ideas and experiences shared in these pages.

Bishop Juan Arzube, Msgr. John Barry, Rev. Ralph Tichenor, S.J., Rev. Patrick Crowley, SS.CC. and Sister Gemma Fisher, S.N.J.M. have each shared a deep awareness of the spiritual hunger of Catholics to enter more fully into their Christian heritage through the study and understanding of God's Word in their daily lives. Since the programs began four years ago each has given us words of advice, encouragement and support at important points along the way.

Rev. John Cooley and Rev. Finbar Devine, SS.CC. were open to new approaches to study, sharing and praying Scripture and let the first parish and area Scripture Programs respectively, be initiated under their guidance. We are most grateful to Rev. Francis MacNutt, O.P. and Rev. Joseph Lange, O.S.F.S., whose sharing opened the "door" for this book to be published.

Our thanks to each one, for we are able to share today in some measure because these friends have helped make these pages possible.

Our heartfelt love and gratitude for each of the members of the home Scripture group, Terry and Chuck Freeman, Elizabeth and Mike Straziuso, Becky and John Campbell, Eileen and Doyle Carlson, Joe De Risio, and Norm Clark whose constant abiding love, faith and hope have so deeply enriched our lives and enabled us to share through God's Word our mutual experience of community with others.

For the generous sharing of their ideas and experiences, we want to give special thanks to Kay Murdy, Mary Girillo, Pat Smolinski, and John Clauder of the Parousia music group. Our appreciation to all the Scripture Program participants these past four years who have generously shared their personal faith-experiences of God's love and thereby demonstrated the real "fruit" of their studying, sharing and praying Scripture together in the programs.

A very special thanks to Caroline Olague who so cheerfully typed the final manuscript. A special gift!

Our joyful thanksgiving to our children, each of whom has shown patience, understanding, cooperation and support during the time we spent on the final manuscript.

"All we love deeply becomes part of us" . . . and these and the many others who have shared their lives with us in so many ways have truly become "part of us," enabling us to share their gifts to us with others. God bless you all in the abundant measure we've felt blessed by your presence in our lives.

And most of all, to my coauthor, "editor," closest friend and helpmate through twenty-five years of marriage, who has so often called forth new gifts in me and generously shared his/her gifts with me, until they have flowed together into our gift for others. We praise and thank God!

Dianne and Roger Miller
December 8, 1978

FOREWORD

A Scripture course for Catholics is certainly the fulfillment of a need that has been growing since Vatican II. The present course has the advantage of having been tested successfully for some years in various parishes and has proven most successful. It is modern, evangelical, and Catholic and is aimed at parishes and small groups. Those who have used it have been high in its praise and many have taken up the work of teaching the Scripture because of the confidence they gained while sharing and learning in study groups.

Mr. and Mrs. Roger Miller have worked and prayed and consulted to make this book worthy of the Lord, whom they love and honor. Their background in education and especially C.C.D. gave them an advantage as they were able to relate to the concrete needs of Catholic people.

I have been waiting for this book and praying for it a long time now. It is a joy to have been able to share, even as slightly as I have, in seeing it brought to fruition. I am not a prophet, but I can see much good coming from this course of study.

Ralph T. Tichenor, S.J.
President, Southern California
Renewal Communities

INTRODUCTION

In recent years, catechesis and adult education have taken on a new and exciting relationship. The Church has issued a very clear call to all involved in catechetical ministry to have continuing adult formation as their first priority.

Roger and Dianne Miller have very courageously responded to this call. They have recognized the hunger of so many in our Catholic community for a deeper understanding of God's Word and have done something concrete about it. They used their own gift of facilitating group study and the work of various scholars to help many have a deeper appreciation of Sacred Scripture. Their key to success has been simplicity of approach and an openness to working closely with local parish communities in the formation of group leaders.

There are many resources suggested in this book. They should be used with the awareness that the intent of the program is always to deepen respect and love for God's Word. Our final guidance is always the authentic interpretation given to us by the Church.

A closer examination of this program will show that prayer is an integral part of every meeting. There is always a deep respect for the unique growth processes of each individual and an opportunity for sharing in a truly Christian atmosphere. This contribution to adult education is a joyous response to the challenge of the Second Vatican Council.

This sacred Synod earnestly and specifically urges all the Christian faithful to learn by frequent reading of the divine Scriptures the "excelling knowledge of Jesus Christ" (Phil. 3:8). "For ignorance of the Scriptures is ignorance of Christ." Therefore, they should gladly put themselves in touch with the sacred text itself, whether it be through the liturgy, rich in the divine word, or through devotional reading, or through instructions suitable for the purpose and other aids which, in our time, are commendably available everywhere, thanks to the approval and active support of the shepherds of the Church. And let them remember that prayer should accompany the reading of sacred Scripture, so that God and man may talk together; for "we speak to Him when we pray; we hear Him when we read the divine sayings."

Rev. Msgr. John F. Barry
Los Angeles Archdiocesan Director,
Religious Education

Chapter 1
MEETING CHRIST IN SCRIPTURE

During recent years it has become increasingly evident that there is a growing desire within God's people to enter more deeply into the study of Scripture. An outgrowth of this desire for solid Catholic teaching is the longing to share with another how the words of Scripture "speak" to us in our daily living. Also evident is the desire to grow in our relationship with God through learning to pray using His Holy Word—the Scriptures.

In the Los Angeles area a very simple Scripture Program has been in operation both in homes and at parish levels for several years. The program has been presented under the co-sponsorship of the Los Angeles Archdiocesan Adult Religious Education Office and the Southern California Renewal Communities (SCRC). The format consists of a three-phased meeting wherein participants study, share and pray Scripture in small groups.

GOALS

The goal of this Scripture Program is:

1) To provide an opportunity for participants to deepen their understanding and knowledge of Scripture through the use of good Catholic teachings provided by qualified speakers, taped talks, audio-visual media and supplemented by home reading.

2) To provide the catalyst within small group sharing that enables participants to find the application of the words of Scripture in their daily lives and to subsequently develop Christian community within their sharing-groups.

3) To provide the opportunity for small group praying of Scripture that contributes to the growth of the individual's personal relationship with Jesus Christ.

4) To encourage the participants to evangelize, i.e., "to go forth" spreading the Good News of God's love with renewed love, concern and service to their families, parishes and communities.

This book will outline a very successful, yet simple format for home and parish Scripture programs. Special emphasis will be given to the myriad of excellent Catholic biblical resource material available in the form of taped talks, films, filmstrips with records or cassettes, video tapes, commentaries, study-guides, as well as numerous scriptural enrichment books. Emphasis will also be given to the value of sharing or verbalizing our personal understanding and reflections of a scriptural teaching or taped presentation. Sharing not only allows us to deepen and clarify our understanding of the material at hand, but it helps us to build rapport and community within our small sharing groups. Finally, considerable explanation will be devoted to singularly the most important part of the program—**scriptural praying**. One of the oldest methods of prayer, one used by the Desert Fathers of the early Church, was to read, reflect and pray upon the Scriptures. Succeeding chapters will describe how God's holy Word can be used to formulate and verbalize rich prayers of praise, petition, thanksgiving, contrition and adoration.

This approach to Scripture study has been particularly successful in utilizing the gifted talents of lay people as both organizers and program leaders. Subsequent chapters will demonstrate that the laity do possess the talents, competency and resources necessary to organize and lead home and parish Scripture Programs. Many of our lay people are extremely well qualified also to provide the scriptural teachings.

A CONCEPT OF RELIGIOUS ADULT EDUCATION

As indicated earlier, the program format consists of a three-phased meeting wherein participants **study, share and pray Scripture in small sharing groups**. The development of this format has evolved out of the expressed needs and desires of the participants. Our experience has been that this combined threefold approach of study, and small group sharing and praying, is the catalyst that frees the participants to experience the fruits of authentic religious adult education in their everyday lives! Such religious education is much more than an informational head-trip. It touches the whole person, mind and heart, intellect and attitudes, and totally molds his/her life as a Christian.

The knowledge that comes from solid input and the opportunity for either quiet personal reflection or group reflections through faith-sharing and discussion, helps us to identify with the knowledge received. This identification enables us to assimilate that part of the knowledge that resonates within our own life situations—an experience of renewed and deepened faith. The assimilation draws forth a personal faith-response, letting the head-knowledge become heart-knowledge—"putting on the mind of Jesus Christ." Our prayer motivates us to begin to live out of what we are learning and experiencing, as God's Word gradually affects our life-responses and educates our attitudes as maturing Christians.

Chapter 2
STUDY, SHARE AND PRAY SCRIPTURE

A TYPICAL MEETING

A typical meeting begins with an hour "input" by means of a speaker or taped-talk presentation, augmented by the participant's prior home reading. This is the **STUDY phase** of the meeting.

The subsequent forty-five minutes are devoted to shared discussions within small groups of up to ten persons seated around tables in the parish hall (or in a home environment), and assisted by a team of discussion leader-facilitators. The subject matter of the study presentation provides material for discussion about its biblical meaning (literary, historical, theological and spiritual), as well as its personal application in our individual lives. This is the **SHARING phase** of the meeting.

The last half hour is a form of extemporaneous Scripture praying on a passage compatible with the theme of the **STUDY phase** of the meeting. Following brief introductory-comments, the passage is read to the entire assembly; a minute or two of reflective silence follows the reading and then the individuals within each sharing group express how the passage has personally "spoken" to them in their lives. The passage is read a second time, again followed by a reflective silence and again personally shared within each group. After the third reading of the passage and silent reflection, the participants begin to formulate verbal prayers based upon the passage, in prayers of petition, thanksgiving, praise, etc. This is the **PRAYING SCRIPTURE phase** of the meeting.

STUDY PHASE OF A MEETING

The first phase of a meeting provides the study input upon which the subsequent phases of sharing and praying Scripture are developed. This three-phased format is equally adaptable with any type of study input, as well as any size group or age level, youth to senior citizen.

The main objective in the selection of the type of input is to maintain the continuity of the chosen theme over a period of time. Completely disjointed talks may be entertaining but are not necessarily conducive to spiritual growth within your group. Our most successful program series (six to twelve meetings) have always utilized a selection of talks that have maintained a theme. The series theme can be as general as an Old or New Testament overview, or as specific as a particular prophet, epistle or Gospel. Continuity is the important factor!

A regular speaker is the ideal source of the study input and can easily develop a chosen theme over a period of meetings. When a speaker is not available there are commercially available a sufficient number of taped Scripture talks for a program to continue for many years without duplication of material. Other study aids include audio-visual media (films, filmstrips with records or cassettes, slide sets) and various creative approaches to ingroup reporting and teaching. These study aids can be used in place of, or in addition to, the basic study input provided normally by the speaker or the taped talk. The proliferation of Scripture commentaries, study guides and enrichment books written for the general reader is exciting! Both the beginning and advanced biblical student can find abundant printed material on solid Catholic scriptural teaching. Regular assigned home reading by the program participants always makes a meaningful contribution to the study and sharing phases of any meeting. Finally, the advent of video tapes and diocesan instructional T.V. (I.T.V.) are showing promise of additional potential for study input resources for both home and parish Scripture programs of the future.

Refer to the Resources in the last chapter for detailed listings of books, taped talks, audio-visual media and video tapes currently available for Scripture program enrichment. Catalogues can be requested from the distributors and publishers to provide annual updated resource listings.

SCRIPTURE PROGRAM SPEAKERS

A speaker adds a unique dimension to any meeting and is always appreciated by program members. Question and answer periods after the speaker's presentation and/or after the sharing phase add further enrichment. We have found that letting the speaker know that it is possible to substitute a taped talk in the event a conflict or emergency arises on the scheduled meeting date, is often appreciated by the speaker when making his/her commitment to give a presentation. Stipends are usually given in appreciation of the speaker's contribution to the program.

REGULAR SPEAKERS FOR AN ENTIRE SERIES

As already mentioned, the opportunity of having a speaker who will regularly give the study input for an entire series is ideal! We encourage program leaders to look expectantly within their own parish family for the talented and qualified person among their priests, religious and laity, who may be just waiting to be invited into a Scripture Program as a regular speaker or teacher.

After extending such an invitation, program leaders should arrange a meeting with the prospective speaker to explain fully:

(a) the program format of study, share and praying Scripture within small groups;

(b) that the speaker's role is to provide the study input and does not involve program organization and administration;

(c) the responsibilities of the program leaders in coordinating and leading the meetings.

As the teacher for an entire series, the speaker will usually select the theme to be developed and the books that would provide supportive home study for his/her presentations. Program leaders may wish to offer theme suggestions for the speaker's consideration, e.g., an introductory overview of the Old and/or New Testaments, if a first year program; or a specific theme that participants may have requested, if it is an ongoing program.

The program leaders should share with the prospective speaker the value of prepared home reading guides for the participant's use. Request the speaker to prepare (two to three weeks in advance of each meeting) home reading guide information based on the content of his/her teachings. A sample reading guide information form, with explanation, is included as Appendix A to this chapter. The program leaders arrange for the typing, duplicating and distribution of the appropriate home reading guides prior to each meeting date. (See Appendix G, Chapter 4, for completed sample Home Reading Guides).

GUEST SPEAKERS

Many qualified potential guest speakers are easily located when earnestly sought through our parishes, Catholic high school and college staffs, diocesan religious education office speakers' bureau and Catholic Renewal (Charismatic) Centers, etc. Inquiries for prospective guest speakers will usually bring forth many recommendations and referrals. We have experienced generous cooperation when seeking recommendations, and were greatly encouraged by the number of very fine speakers who were available.

To avoid possible disappointment, it is advisable to contact potential guest speakers three to nine months in advance of the desired date. Initial contact with the guest speaker is preferably made in person or by telephone. Using a letter for the initial contact should be a last resort. At the time of the initial contact, in addition to extending an invitation, the following information should be provided to assist the speaker in making a decision:

(a) An explanation of the Scripture Program format.

(b) The scriptural theme being developed.

(c) Requested topic or choice of topics.

(d) Requested date, or choice of dates.

(e) Explanation of the use and purpose of the Home Reading Guide and the information needed.

After the speaker has accepted the invitation to give a presentation, approximately two months prior to the scheduled visit a letter of confirmation should be sent to the speaker by the program leaders. It should include a restatement of the above points made in the initial contact, and the location of the program meeting with clear directions of how to reach it. Enclose the form for the requested reading guide information (see Appendix A to this chapter). Request return of the completed form three weeks prior to the scheduled program date. If taping is anticipated, it is advisable to include a taping release statement to be signed and also returned.

TAPED TALKS

Taped talks represent a growing resource of Catholic Scripture teachings by renowned speakers and scholars. They are readily available commercially and through local lending tape libraries.

Taped talks can be used most effectively. Our experience using taped talks in groups over a twelve-year period has shown that only one person in ten has any real difficulty with a properly presented taped teaching. Inadequacy of equipment with the resultant loss of an audible presentation, more often than not, contributes most to people's reluctance to use taped material. Encouragement of note taking helps to focus the participant's concentration while listening to the taped talks; and promotes personal participation and shared responsibility during the sharing phase of the meeting.

Two notable benefits of using taped talks are that they can be borrowed and substituted. When members miss a meeting, the taped talk of that meeting can be borrowed, thereby helping them to maintain continuity and interest in the program. If a scheduled speaker has an emergency cancellation, a taped talk can be substituted for the study input and the program continue on as planned. This flexibility of using taped talks in unexpected situations gives greater freedom to program leaders and participants and places less pressure on program speakers.

Many series of taped talks are conducive to good group discussion and sharing. The material available covers the spectrum from basic introductory scriptural talks to some very scholarly commentary style talks for more advanced study groups. We advise program leaders to **preview and evaluate the taped talks** prior to selecting them for use in a particular program situation. The selection of a series of taped talks, or a single taped talk, should be based on:

(1) an awareness of the interests and needs of the members of your Scripture Program;

(2) the receptivity of your members to the material, i.e., basic introductory or more indepth scholarly presentations;

(3) how well the material will stimulate discussion and sharing within your group;

(4) the length of tape (20 to 60 minutes) with which your group will be comfortable;

(5) the length of the taped talk relative to the allotted time of the **STUDY phase** of the meeting;

(6) how suitable the speaker's style and delivery are for group listening, i.e., voice inflection is important since the speaker is not visible;

(7) the audibility and clarity of the tape, i.e., static free, not too much base, sharpness or echo;

(8) the availability of the tapes through lending tape libraries, individual purchase or Scripture Program purchase.

AUDIO-VISUALS FOR STUDY INPUT

Audio-visual media (A-V) can be an effective means of augmenting the study input theme of a Scripture Program series. Selected films or filmstrips with audio accompaniment usually add useful information and a visual experience that touches the emotions and memories of the viewers and stimulates good group sharing.

The importance of previewing the A-V by the program leaders cannot be understated. Previewing offers the opportunity to determine if a particular A-V is appropriate for the program theme, where to place it within the series and how to use it most effectively.

Many places that regularly use religious audio-visuals permit individuals to arrange to come in and spend time previewing the audio-visuals before they arrange to borrow or rent them. Places to contact about previewing arrangements would include: local parish religious education (C.C.D.) resource centers or libraries, Catholic high school libraries, Catholic college libraries or media-centers, diocesan religious education office media-centers or resource centers, Catholic hospital libraries and local audio-visual distributors' offices (if any are located in your area).

Many A-V's come with prepared study guides, including suggestions for media presentation, preliminary questions before showing the A-V and follow-up questions for group discussion. When the A-V does not have such questions, the program leaders should prepare suitable ones to facilitate the sharing phase of the meeting.

The films and filmstrips that are most suitable for study-input usually vary from twenty to sixty minutes in length. The shorter audio-visuals are most effective when shown a second time as a means of summation after the **SHARING phase** of the meeting; or in the context of prayerful reflection as an introduction to the **PRAYING SCRIPTURE phase** of the meeting.

The content and purpose of the A-V should determine its placement within a series and how it can be most effectively presented. Many A-Vs are beneficially used at a mid-series point to emphasize and develop a specific aspect of the Old or New Testament theme. For example:

"The Exodus" (Mass Media Ministries), "The Passover" (Gospel Films), "Sermon on the Mount" (Mass Media Ministries), "Who is Jesus?" (Paulist Press), "Reconciliation in the Gospel of Matthew" (Paulist Press), "Faith in the Gospel of Mark" (Paulist Press), "Prayer of Jesus in the Gospel of Luke" (Paulist Press), "Eucharist in the Gospel of John" (Paulist Press), "The Conversion" (Cathedral Films), "The Parable" (Mass Media Ministries).

Certain filmstrips offer an overview approach that makes them suitable for use either at the initial program meeting as an introduction to the series' theme or to review and summarize the theme during the concluding meeting of the series. For example . . . .

(a) If the series' theme is an "*Overview of the Old Testament,*" these filmstrips would be an enrichment: "Exodus of Israel" (Alpha-Omega) for the first meeting of the series; and "Exodus of Jesus" (Alpha-Omega) for the last meeting of the series.

(b) If the study of one of the Gospels is the theme to be developed in a series of (6–12) meetings, the following filmstrips could be used either to give the first meeting introductory-overview or the last meeting summary-review: "Matthew—Discipleship," "Mark—Christian Kerygma," "Luke—Prayer and Social Apostolate," "John—Spirituality and Sacrament" from the *Service Evangelists Filmstrip Series* by Paulist Press; "The Gospel According to Matthew," "The Gospel According to Mark," "The Gospel According to Luke," "The Gospel According to John" from *The Four Gospels Filmstrip Series* by Alba House.

(c) If the series' theme is the *"Overview of the New Testament,"* the filmstrips listed under "b" above could also be used at a meeting preceding or following a speaker's presentation (or a taped talk) on a specific Gospel.

A film or slide presentation on the Holy Land can be an opportunity to visually experience the meaning of the words we've been reading and sharing as well as a means of familiarization with the places where the biblical events occurred. There are excellent films (up to an hour in length) on the land of the Bible. Several are listed in the last chapter under audio-visual resources, but one can also inquire about borrowing or renting Holy Land films through local travel agencies and airlines (KLM has an outstanding film).

We've had the good fortune to have program members share their own slides and personal reflections of their visits to Israel. Each presentation was given at the end of a program year as a wrap-up for a series. One presentation was arranged in the sequence of the mysteries of the rosary and related Scripture verses were read as slides were viewed of the events of our Lord's life. Another presentation geographically covered many of the locations where the great themes of the Old and New Testament had occurred. The personal impressions shared by the Holy Land visitors, as they showed their slides, made these meetings not only informative, but personally meaningful for all in the program.

SCRIPTURE COMMENTARIES, STUDY GUIDES AND ENRICHMENT BOOKS

There is no substitute for the daily reading, study and praying of Scripture. Regular assigned Scripture readings for home study and prayer are a part of the program format and an essential preparation for each meeting. Additional home reading from Scripture commentary or study guide books can enhance the individual's understanding of the THEN-context of the Scripture.

Since 1974 the number of good Catholic Scripture study and enrichment books written for the general reader has more than tripled. It is possible to select any biblical theme for study and be able to choose complementary reading from a variety of Scripture commentaries, study guides and enrichment books.

Parish Scripture Program participants' requests for home-study aids have resulted in the development of "home reading guides" (see an example in Chapter 4, Appendix G).

Such guides have been appreciated and found to be most beneficial by those participants desiring guidelines for more comprehensive home study. In addition to the assigned Scripture readings, for a forthcoming meeting the "guides" also suggest complementary readings from "basic" commentary books wherein chapters and pages are listed that are pertinent to the meeting's theme.

Program members are encouraged to take advantage of as much background home study as they can find possible. Reading is suggested from two or three "basic" books simultaneously because of various writing styles that reach the needs of different readers. The participants choose which books they prefer for their home reading. Additional books that provide enriching insights on specific themes of Scripture are also suggested for those members wanting further personal scriptural enrichment.

When program leaders or speakers select specific commentaries, study guides and enrichment books for recommended home study, they should take into consideration the program memberships' previous scriptural study, background (beginning, advanced or intermediate) and educational level (high school youth group or adult program). Most programs will probably contain a cross section of people representing varied backgrounds and interests. This is another reason for recommending two or three "basic" books for each series' theme.

Refer to Book Resources in the last chapter for an extensive listing of Scripture study commentaries, study guides and enrichment books on specific biblical themes. Refer to Chapter 4, for suggested series themes and related resources.

VIDEO CASSETTE TAPES AND INSTRUCTIONAL T.V.

Two exciting means of study input that are becoming more readily available are video tapes and diocesan instructional T.V. (I.T.V.). The most common objection raised by the ten percent who find difficulty using (audio) taped talks is that they have no visual focus to hold their attention. Video tapes and I.T.V. are an answer to that objection.

Some of the first Catholic Scripture video tape teachings were made at the Catholic Charismatic Bible Institute held at St. Mary's University in San Antonio, Texas during the summer of 1978. Four Scripture presentations covered six topics totalling fifty-eight video tapings. We had had an opportunity to preview several video tape teachings by each of the speakers and we were excited about their potential for use in both home and parish programs. The topics, speakers and subject matter are listed in the resource chapter under the audio-visual video-tape section. In future years we can expect that the variety and availability of Scripture teachings on video tapes will make them one of the more popular means of Scripture study input.

Video tapes are an ideal study input for a home Scripture program. The video cassette deck jacked into the family T.V. provides an effective means of presentation in a comfortable, relaxed environment. One feels it is almost like having the speaker in the same room! After the video-taped presentation, the group sharing is facilitated by the program leaders with the use of prepared discussion questions based on the lecture content. Selection of a Scripture passage complementary to the theme of the lecture is used for the praying phase.

Video tapes are also adaptable for the study input in a parish Scripture Program. The tapes can be used either with a video cassette deck jacked into a standard or enlarged T.V. screen in the parish hall or lounge, or else through the diocesan I.T.V. facilities using the parish's T.V. sets in the classrooms, lounge or hall. The program format of studying, sharing and praying Scripture is followed the same as with other types of study input materials or speakers. A reminder, if all the participants must group together to conveniently view the video-tape presentation, it is important at its conclusion that they return to their assigned table groups for the sharing and praying phases of the meeting. The table discussion leaders facilitate the group discussion using prepared discussion questions. The program leaders also select a compatible passage for praying Scripture. The opportunity for adequate small group sharing and prayer is the important catalyst that can make the video-tape lecture a successful study input for Scripture programs.

Where the video tapes are used with a parish's own video cassette deck and T.V. there is greater scheduling flexibility as to choice of topics, program time (daytime or nighttime) and the day of the week for the meetings.

Parishes that have diocesan I.T.V. facilities will find their program time more predetermined and restricted to the scheduled video tape airing from the central diocesan studios. An advantage to this means of study input is that many parish programs can simultaneously benefit from a single video presentation. For example, the Los Angeles Archdiocese has ninety parishes with I.T.V. facilities and a centrally located studio from which the video tapes, or live presentations are aired. Through the diocesan department of communication and the religious education office, single presentations and/or a series of teachings are coordinated, publicized and offered to all parishes that participate in the I.T.V. program.

For Parish Scripture Programs that wish to use this study input approach, there must be prearranged scheduling of the video-tape broadcasts to benefit to the greatest extent possible all the participating parishes. An ideal leadership approach is to have the program leaders of a parish program take the initiative of coordinating all the basic arrangements: the choice of theme, program meeting day and time, and the scheduling of the video-tape broadcasts with the appropriate diocesan offices and departments. Other Parish Scripture Program leaders in the diocese may then be contacted to inquire if they are interested in benefiting from the scheduled I.T.V. series.

Another approach is for all the interested parish program leaders in the diocese to meet and mutually choose a theme, decide on acceptable meeting day(s) and time(s), coordinate program publicity within the diocese and their parishes, and arrange for the scheduled airing of the video tapes through the diocesan I.T.V. studio.

One of the many exciting prospects of using the diocesan I.T.V. facilities is that diocesan-sponsored live Scripture teachings could also be scheduled regularly for both daytime and nighttime Scripture programs in the diocese. What a tremendous potential for evangelization within our parishes, not only through Scripture studies, but through all areas of interest in Catholic adult religious education!

SHARING PHASE OF THE MEETING

The second part of a typical meeting is a discussion and **SHARING phase** wherein members verbalize their personal understanding of the study input portion of the meeting. Sharing deepens and clarifies understanding and builds rapport within the group. As trust grows community forms and group members are able to share openly with one another.

TEAM LEADERSHIP

Team leadership provides mutual support for facilitating the discussions. The discussion leaders' tasks are to keep the discussion on the topic of the meeting. They are "enablers" of discussion, not instructors or teachers. During the **SHARING phase**, the discussion leaders can also share their comments, their own reflections, feelings and questions. Another value in team leadership is one team member can carry on in the absence of a co-leader.

DISCUSSION SHARING QUESTIONS

Prepared study and reflection type questions contribute toward the discussion of the biblical meaning of the material as well as encouraging personal faith sharing among the participants.

Two kinds of questions are helpful:

(1) **Informative questions** that develop an awareness and understanding of the scriptural background of the material being studied. These study type questions should be applied to the **THEN-context** of the Scripture theme, passage, or subject.

(2) **Formative questions** that focus awareness on how the study material is applicable to the lives of the participants today. These reflective type questions should be applied to the **NOW-context** of the Scripture theme, passage, or subject.

Four to six questions are sufficient for a given meeting. The first two or three should be informative questions and the latter should be formative questions, so that group sharing always progresses from head-knowledge to heart-knowledge of God's Word in Scripture. Either stated questions or declarative statements for discussion (i.e., "discuss the meaning of . . .") are suitable.

Sources for such questions vary with the selection of the study material used. Sources include:

(1) **Study guides** (books) usually have study questions at the end of each chapter. When there are no "formative" questions listed they should be formulated by the program or discussion leaders prior to the meeting.

(2) **Audio-visuals** (films, filmstrips, video tapes) and taped talks usually have corresponding study guides that include questions. If no "formative" questions are included, the program leaders should compose them when they preview the material prior to the meeting.

(3) **Speakers** (regular or guest) are usually very willing to compose both kinds of questions based on the content of their teaching, when asked sufficiently in advance of their presentation date, i.e., one to two months beforehand.

(4) **Program leaders** preparation of questions as they preview taped talks or other audio-visuals are always helpful, especially when the selected media does not include prepared study guides with study or reflection questions.

(5) **Participants'** own "notes" taken as they listen to presentations can be a source of excellent "informative" and "formative" questions and these are always especially pertinent to the interests of the listener.

In the Scripture Program the primary purpose of the informative questions is that they should always lead to formative questions that culminate in the participants' reflection on the Scriptures' personal application in their individual lives.

It is through the personal faith-sharings of the members, enlightened by the study of the Scriptures, that they enable one another to experience the reality of the "living" Word of God within their own lives. Through this approach of study and sharing Scripture many people have experienced the Scriptures becoming "alive" and meaningful for them in their daily lives.

PRAYING SCRIPTURE PHASE OF THE MEETING

The **Praying Scripture phase** of the meeting (as in times of personal prayer with Scripture) is a listening to God who speaks to us personally in his written Word. During this phase of the meeting, praying Scripture is a blend of both personal prayer and community shared prayer. Scripture becomes a "Living Word" personally heard and shared with others in the context of a faith-filled loving community.

One of the oldest known methods of prayer that was used by the Desert Fathers was to read, reflect and pray upon the Scriptures. The threefold-reading approach to scriptural prayer, as used in this Scripture Program, is adapted from a method we first read in an article, *"A Suggestion for Shared Praying of Scripture"* by Rev. Armand M. Nigro, S.J. (article #120—Gonzaga University, Spokane, Wash.) and later described by David Rosage, S.J. in his book *"Discovering Pathways to Prayer"* and his taped-talk, *"Brotherhood: A New Way of Living-Praying Scripture."*

METHOD USED INITIALLY TO INTRODUCE SCRIPTURE PRAYING IN SMALL GROUPS

A passage is selected that is compatible with the theme of the talk heard in the study phase of the meeting. The length of the passage is usually held to between five and fifteen verses. One of the program leaders introduces the passage to the group with some of the suggested "aids" listed later in this chapter, which provide the background context of the passage and suggest ways of personalizing it within our own lives. The leader uses symbolisms, analogies and/or questions that help the participants to hear the passage in relationship to their own present life situations.

FIRST READING

The passage is read to the entire group. Following the first reading all quietly reflect for a few minutes upon the Word, meditating or contemplating, as desired. The group then begins to share with their respective members what the Word is "saying" to them personally. **The sharing is kept personal.** The sharing is not "we," "they," or "those"; ***it is what "I" hear personally from the passage as it is applied to my life today;*** "This passage says to me . . ." or "what I hear in this verse is . . . ." This is not a time for discussion or commenting on what another has shared, nor is it advice-giving time. The program leaders discern when the first sharing should end and the second reading should begin. (Sharing lasts between five and ten minutes.)

SECOND READING

The passage is read a second time for the group. All participants quietly meditate on the Word before beginning to share what additional insights the Lord has given them. Because of the previous readings and sharing the passage will have more meaning, deeper insights, and bring alive new levels of hearing and awareness of the Word. (Sharing session again lasts about five to ten minutes.)

THIRD READING

The passage is now read for the third time, reflected upon, and this time the participants pray the Scripture. That is, they formulate spontaneous prayers of praise, petition, thanksgiving, contrition, adoration, etc. At this time all participants are encouraged to verbalize their own prayers out loud within the group. No sharing is done at this time; and no comments or discussion is made of another member's prayer. The shared praying continues for from five to ten minutes, and is brought to a close with an "Amen" by the program leaders.

It takes time and experience for people to become comfortable and open enough to share their personal thoughts, feelings and prayers with one another; therefore, at the beginning of the program allow three to five minutes after each reading for the reflection and sharing time. As a group matures, they will automatically want to spend more time praying. The need then will be to limit the overall length of time in order to stay within the total meeting schedule.

We need to become comfortable with periods of silence. Silence does not have to be filled with back-to-back sharings. Silence is in itself "OK!" As St. John of the Cross expressed it . . . "The language that God hears best is the silent language of Love."

HELPFUL ATTITUDES AND APPROACHES WHEN PRAYING SCRIPTURE

Group leaders need to be patient, encouraging, gentle, supportive and understanding as they share how to pray with Scripture. It takes time, maybe months, before new patterns of sharing and praying together are comfortable for everyone in a group. The following are various suggestions that leaders may find helpful to share with their groups:

(1) When praying Scripture **let go of the literal meaning of words, find the symbolism in the passage and the analogy to our own lives**. Christ taught this way in his parables: e.g., the "seed" was symbolic to the "Word of God," and the "wedding feast" was analogous to the "Kingdom of God."

The story of Zacchaeus (Lk. 19:1–10), rich in symbolism and analogy, has meaning for us today. Zacchaeus climbed a sycamore tree to see Christ and his life was changed! How are we like Zacchaeus?

Zacchaeus was small in stature and had accepted his physical limitations. Where am I "small in stature?" Do I accept myself as God accepts me, as I am at this moment in all areas of my life?

Zacchaeus climbed a sycamore tree to help him to see Christ. Do I look for opportunities to "climb" and grow to help me to see Christ in my life? What ways could I "climb" today? What or who are the "sycamore trees" of my life?

Zacchaeus' response to Christ was spontaneous, immediate, delighted and total. What is my response in the NOW-moments of my life?

(2) **Personalize the passage as much as possible. Put your own name in the context of the passage,** and where possible **put in the names of family members,** your life situations, personal circumstances, concerns, joys, etc.

(a) In the Old Testament **put your own name wherever the names of Israel, Jacob and Jerusalem are used,** such as in Isaiah 43–44. See how your life journey of faith parallels the faith journey of the Israelites as they received the covenant promise, repeatedly broke and renewed it during their exodus and desert experiences, and into the promised land. Hear anew, God's promise of faithfulness today to you, as it was to them, and as it still is throughout the life journey of faith.

(b) **Put your name in the place of a prophet,** such as in the cries of *Jeremiah* (15:18, 17:14, 20:7–12) in times of distress, and "hear" God's message to Jeremiah at the potter's house (18:1–10).

(c) **In the events of Christ's life, put yourself in the scenes and participate in the event. Imagine** how the people involved must have felt and how they responded. How would you respond in their place? **Listen to Christ speaking personally to you** through his parables and sermons. What is your response?

(3) **Background reading is an important aid in praying Scripture.** Read a biblical commentary on the text chosen for prayer. In light of the THEN-context of the passage, "hear" what God in his Word may be saying to you in the NOW-context of your life. **Ask such basic questions** as "what, where, when, why, how and who."

(4) **Underline meaningful passages or jot down insights** that come during prayer. These notes can be kept in a Scripture-Prayer Journal or written in the margins of your Bible. Over a period of time such journal or margin notes reveal how God is faithfully meeting us at our point of need—leading us to himself through his Word.

(5) **It is important to read the passage out loud** when praying Scripture alone. "Hear" the Word of God addressed to you personally!

(6) Following are some excellent passages that may be used as Scripture-prayer starters.

Old Testament Passages:
Isaiah 43, Isaiah 55, Psalms 1, 23, 27, 84, 91, 139.

Christ's Parables:
Mark 4:1–25, Matthew 25:31–46, Luke 10:25–37.

Events in Christ's Life:
Matthew 5:1–16, Luke 6:27–47, Mark 6:45–51, Mark 4:35–41, John 11:1–44, John 15–17, Mark 14:32–42, Luke 24:13–35.

Paul's Letters:
1 Corinthians 13:1–13, Galatians 5:13–26, Ephesians 4:1–16, Philemon 3:7–16, Colossians 3:12–17, 2 Timothy 3:10–17.

SOME ADDITIONAL VARIATIONS OF THE PRAYING SCRIPTURE METHOD

Following are some of the many variations we have found most useful and enriching in either group Scripture praying or in private times of praying Scripture. Once a group is comfortable and familiar with the initial basic method of praying Scripture together, a variation can be introduced with a brief explanation of how it is adapted to the basic threefold approach of praying Scripture. Some of the variations are adaptable for either group use or for use during private times of personal prayer. Approaches #5, #6 and #7 are best suited for, and directed to, individual private times of praying Scripture.

Initial Method that is the Basis of Other Variations

First Reading . . . Reflection . . . Sharing,

Second Reading . . . Reflection . . . Sharing,

Third Reading . . . Reflection . . . Praying.

Variation No. 1
(Adapted from a Celtic Meditation described by Rev. Edward Farrell in his book *Prayer Is A Hunger.*)

First Reading . . . Silent Reflection period (only, no verbal sharing),

Second Reading . . . Writing, in silence, out of one's reflection,

Third Reading . . . Sharing within group, based on what has been written, and this can often flow into praying also.

This approach often frees the more quiet participants to feel comfortable and enables them to verbalize within the group. The "praying" is personal and private, done during the silent reflection and writing time. The "writing" can be expressed as poetry, a journal entry, a letter to Christ, a prayer, etc. "Sharing" follows the time of personal reflection, praying and silent writing. (Allow five to ten minutes after the first and second readings; allow twice as long after the third reading for all who wish to share from their written reflections.)

Variation No. 2
(Adapted from a Celtic Meditation in *Prayer Is A Hunger*, without writing.)

First Reading . . . Silent listening-prayer and reflection (no verbal sharing),

Second Reading . . . Reflection on the NOW-context of **passage** . . . Personal sharing,

Third Reading . . . Reflection . . . Praying within group.

The period of planned silence after the first reading, with no verbal sharing, enables prayerful "listening" of the Word. Extended personal sharing time after the second reading encourages fuller participation and sharing before the third reading and the praying within the group. This approach is especially effective for beginning adult Scripture-sharing groups and for youth groups. It allows for greater listening and reflection time as well as extended sharing time and leads to greater ease and freedom in shared prayer within the group.

Variation No. 3
(Adapted from "informative-formative" explanation of reading Scripture by Rev. Adrian Van Kaam in his book *Woman at the Well*.)

First Reading . . . Reflection on Basic Questions of the THEN-context . . . Sharing,

Second Reading . . . Reflection on Basic Questions of the NOW-context . . . Sharing,

Third Reading . . . Reflection Time . . . Praying within group.

The basic questions "what, when, where, why, how and who" are asked after the first reading in the THEN-context of the passage; after the second reading the questions are again asked in the NOW-context of the passage—that is how it affects one's own life today. This approach provides for both informative and formative reflection. After the first reading share how **you personally** understand the background of the passage, that is how you feel those in the passage must have felt or reacted. This is not an exegetic study approach, but a personal-feeling approach.

Variation No. 4
(Adapted from Marriage Encounter Dialogue Technique.)

First Reading . . . Silent Reflection on Question . . . Sharing,
Questions: "What is the message/meaning God gives in this passage?" "How do I imagine/think Jesus would feel about this message?"

Second Reading . . . Silent Reflection on Question . . . Sharing,
Questions: "How do I feel about the message/meaning I 'hear' in this passage?" "How do I feel about this passage in application to my life (or our life, as a couple) today?"

Third Reading . . . Silent Reflection Time . . . Praying within group (as a couple).

Between a couple or in a group, this approach is used with time allowed for writing responses (one question at a time) before each sharing begins.

Variation No. 5
(Adapted for private time of praying with Scripture.)

First Reading . . . Reflection Time . . . Cross-reference reading of related passages,

Second Reading . . . Reflection Time . . . Writing,

Third Reading . . . Reflection Time . . . that flows into personal prayer.

When praying Scripture alone read the passage aloud—it is important to "hear" the Word. Cross reference reading of related passages listed in the Scriptures enriches meaning and furthers understanding of the interrelationship between the Old and New Testament passages. After a period of quiet reflection write your thoughts. When alone, quiet reflection and writing are effective means of "sharing." New levels of "hearing" in the heart are touched by the Spirit.

Variation No. 6
(Adapted primarily for private indepth study, sharing and praying of Scripture.)

First Reading . . . Cross-reference reading of related passages . . . Reflection,

Second Reading . . . Questions on the THEN-context . . . Reflection . . . Writing,

Third Reading . . . Commentary readings relating to the passage . . . Reflection,

Fourth Reading . . . Questions on the NOW-context—one's own life . . . Reflection,

Fifth Reading . . . Reflection . . . Writing,

Sixth Reading . . . Prayer . . . flowing into Resting in the Presence of the Living Word!

This is an effective and enriching approach—allowing Scripture to form oneself into the likeness of Christ through his Word. The cross-reference reading, reflective questioning, commentary reading and writing are each expressions of praying Scripture which can lead one to the prayer of simply being in the Presence of the Word.

Variation No. 7
(Adapted to use with the Sunday Liturgical Readings.)

Monday . . . Read and pray all four passages to understand the overall theme conveyed.

Tuesday . . . Read and pray the Old Testament passage.

Wednesday . . . Read and pray the Psalm.

Thursday . . . Read and pray the Epistle passage.

Friday . . . Read and pray the Gospel passage.

Saturday . . . Again read and pray all four passages as parts of the whole overall liturgical theme for the Sunday Liturgy Readings.

This suggested variation which develops a thematic daily approach to praying Scripture enables the Sunday readings to come "alive" in a new way because one has lived with them during the week!

Enrichment Books for Praying Scripture

The *Bible* itself, when read and studied reflectively with a "listening heart," is the perfect God-given Prayer Book! Cross-referencing of related passages heightens one's appreciation and understanding of any single passage and contributes to the overview of the continuity of the Word of God through the Old and New Testaments.

Biblical Commentaries and *Scripture Reading Guides* can also provide rich and detailed background for insights when praying Scripture.

Concordances and *Topical Bible Indexes* are helpful for the thematic development of a passage with other related passages in Scripture.

Selected *Enrichment Books* offer guidance and inspiration in learning how to read, study and pray Scripture. Refer to the resources listed in the last chapter for a specialized list of books suitable for background preparation and personal enrichment in the praying of Scripture.

AUDIO VISUAL AIDS TO BE USED WITH VARIATIONS IN PRAYING SCRIPTURE

Cassettes—Biblical Meditations with Music

A short (2–5 minute) narrative introduction of a Scripture passage invites the listener to become personally involved with the biblical characters and events. Following each narration, specially selected classical music is provided by the cassette to enhance meditation.

These narrative-music cassettes are effective aids with scriptural praying Variation No. 1 and No. 2, or when privately praying Scripture. Use the narrative introduction and music after the first reading of the passage. Writing (Variation No. 1) can be done either during the music or at its conclusion. Sharing (Variation No. 2) follows the Scripture reading or after the music ends. Refer to the resources in the last chapter for a listing of the cassettes and their sources.

Recorded Songs Based on Scripture Passages

Playing songs based on Scripture passages during the "reflection-prayer" time after the first reading (or other readings) are enriching meditational aids. The selected song should complement the chosen Scripture passage to be prayed. The songs can be used with the basic method or any of the variations for scriptural prayer, either in groups or privately. Refer to the Resources in the last chapter for a listing of recorded albums comprising songs based on Scripture.

Films, Filmstrips and Slide Sets for Scripture Prayer

The audio-visual media is a powerful aid to use in the **PRAYING SCRIPTURE phase** of a meeting. A wide variety of suitable films, filmstrips and slide sets are available in lengths varying from two-minute inspirational films (TeleSPOTS) to twenty-minute filmstrips on contemporary parables. The key factor in the selection and method of presenting audio-visual media as an aid to scriptural prayer is that it should lead the viewers into prayerful reflection rather than a study type discussion. Audio-visuals should always be previewed beforehand to be sure that they will complement and develop the theme of the meeting and the Scripture passage selected for prayer.

The audio-visual media can be mood setters for prayer, from visual-narratives conducive to meditative reflections that enhance the group sharing and prayer, to simply those conducive to silent visual meditations. When possible a repeat showing of the media is most effective, such as after the first Scripture reading and again after the third reading just before group prayer. Keeping the lights dimmed during the entire period of sharing and prayer often contributes to a prayerful atmosphere. Encourage periods of reflective, prayerful silence immediately following the presentations before moving into the next reading, sharing or prayer. Quite often it takes a little time to assimilate the impact an audio-visual aid can produce in a prayerful environment.

Slide series that develop a visual theme or set a mood are also useful aids in Scripture prayers. Slides can be accompanied by recorded narration, selected classical music, a slow reflective reading of the selected Scripture passage, or simply viewing the slides in meditative silence. As with the use of other audio-visual aids, the slide series, or selected portions of it, can be presented again after (or during) the third Scripture reading. If a recorded narration was used with the first presentation, Scripture reading, music or silence during the second showing can be most effective.

Examples of the Use of Audio-Visuals

Following are some examples of how to use audio-visuals during the *PRAYING SCRIPTURE phase* of a meeting.

Single Showing of Audio-Visual (Film, Filmstrip or Slides)

Use Variation No. 2 for praying Scripture.

First Reading . . . Audio-Visual presentation . . . Reflective Silence,

Second Reading . . . Reflection . . . Personal Sharing within group(s),

Third Reading . . . Reflection . . . Shared prayer within group(s).

Repeated Showing of Audio-Visual

Use Variation No. 2 for praying Scripture.

First Reading . . . Audio-Visual presentation . . . Reflective Silence,

Second Reading . . . Reflection . . . Personal Sharing within group(s),

Third Reading . . . Repeat presentation of audio-visual . . . Reflection, followed by praying within group(s).

ALTERNATIVE METHODS OF PRESENTATION FOR SECOND SHOWING OF AUDIO-VISUAL AIDS

(1) Show the audio-visuals without a soundtrack, accompanied instead by selected classical music that will enhance meditative reflection during the viewing.

(2) When the content of an audio-visual is suitable, during the second showing omit the soundtrack and instead read the Scripture passage slowly and reflectively. Practice beforehand and synchronize the verses to accompany and complement the visual presentation as much as possible.

(3) Show a visual presentation only of the film, filmstrip or slides, and let the silence be the catalyst for deepened visual-meditation.

Adapting A "Study" Audio-Visual for Use in Praying Scripture

It is possible to beneficially use the same audio-visual in the first two phases of the meeting and then adapt it for the *PRAYING SCRIPTURE phase*. When used in this fashion it facilitates the transition of the head-to-heart knowledge of the subject or theme of the meeting. To adapt the "study" audio-visual material for use in praying Scripture, select a two-to-five minute section of the film or filmstrip that focuses in on a single aspect of the meeting theme, or develops a specific point in the Scripture. This selection should complement the Scripture passage to be used for prayer. Present the section of film or filmstrip, without the soundtrack, either after or during the first reading of the Scripture passage. Using Scripture praying Variation No. 2, follow the steps listed for a single showing of an audio-visual aid.

Refer to the Resources in the last chapter for a listing of suitable audio-visual aids that can enhance the *PRAYING SCRIPTURE phase* of a meeting. Distributors and publishers of such materials are also listed.

APPENDIX A
(Page 1 of 2)

SUGGESTED HOME READING GUIDE INFORMATION FORM

Please return this form before (3 weeks before date of scheduled visit)

Mail to: _____
(Program Leader's Name and Address)

Speaker's Name _____

Title of Talk _____

Date and Time _____

SCRIPTURE READING
(Please suggest relevant Scripture for home reading preparation.)

_____

_____

SCRIPTURE PASSAGES
(Please suggest five Scripture passages—5 to 15 verses in length—that could prayerfully amplify the study theme. These passages will be suggested for personal prayer use before the meeting, with one passage to be used during the **PRAYING SCRIPTURE phase** of the meeting.)

_____

_____

_____

_____

_____

QUESTIONS
(Please compose five or six questions or discussion-statements which will be suggested for personal use in home study as well as facilitation-aids during the **SHARING phase** of the meeting. Two kinds of questions are suggested:

1) **Informative Questions** (2 to 3) that will assist the listeners into a deeper understanding of the THEN-context of the Scripture message.

2) **Formative Questions** (3 to 4) that focus awareness on the NOW-context of the Scripture message in application to the listeners' lives today.

_____

_____

_____

_____

_____

_____

_____

_____

DO YOU ANTICIPATE A QUESTION/ANSWER PERIOD? _____

_____

RELEASE FOR YOUR PRESENTATION TO BE TAPED AND MADE AVAILABLE:
I give my permission for my presentation/teaching to be taped, duplicated and made available to Scripture Program participants through loan-out and/or by purchase.
Signed _____

FOR THE PURPOSES OF INTRODUCTION—please state personal and educational background material you would like mentioned.

_____

_____

_____

_____

Chapter 3
HOME SCRIPTURE PROGRAMS

VALUE OF A HOME PROGRAM

Our experience has shown there is real value in beginning small and building community with a core group of dedicated friends. The small group sharing and praying together does build a spirit of community among those participating, and it is the strength and experience of this community that is so vital to successfully organizing and setting-up the larger (parish size) programs.

HOW TO ORGANIZE AND SET-UP A HOME SCRIPTURE PROGRAM

To begin a Home Scripture Program, one need only invite some friends to gather together who are interested in growing closer to the Lord through the study, sharing and praying of his holy Word. A married couple or two persons willing to share responsibilities as a team, are recognized as the program leaders within the group. The meeting is held in their home or a location designated by them. The meeting location should be a fixed place and not rotated from home to home.

At the initial meeting the program purpose and format are explained; the frequency and desired length of meetings are determined. The first-year study theme, sources of study input and books to be used can be predetermined by the program leaders or mutually decided upon by the group. The choice is often directed by the scriptural background knowledge of the members and the resources available to the group.

The resources are almost unlimited. If a qualified Scripture teacher is not available to provide your group study input on a regular basis, then utilize the many taped talks, filmstrips with records or cassettes, films or video tapes listed in the last chapter on resources. Initially one of the easiest sources for the study input (or teaching) will consist of taped scriptural talks using a series of six to ten tapes which follow a scriptural theme.

Whenever possible guests can be invited to give a presentation complementary to the chosen theme of the series, and to participate in the group discussions. For potential guest speakers contact local Catholic high schools and colleges, the diocesan speaker's bureau, adult religious education offices, and of course, the priests and sisters within one's own parish.

When the majority of the participants are beginning Scripture students, the study theme for a first-year program should be an introduction to Scripture through an overview of the Old and New Testaments.

Select appropriate Scripture commentaries and study guides to develop the chosen study theme and to augment the meeting's study input. Assigned home reading, prior to the meeting, will always contribute significantly to each member's participation, enhancing the group's understanding and clarify many questions that may arise.

The leader couple or team should arrange to preview the study material (tapes, audio-visuals, books) beforehand to evaluate them for the needs and interest of their individual group. Questions formulated during the previewing of the tapes can be excellent discussion-starters and used to facilitate the **SHARING phase** of the meeting.

From the second year on, more indepth and specialized thematic subject material can be chosen, such as a series on the Prophets, a Gospel, an Epistle, etc. Members should share individually in previewing various tapes and then mutually choose the succeeding year's Scripture themes and material for the **STUDY phase**.

In the event tapes are played, the equipment should be of a sufficient size and capability that will ensure clear and audible reproduction of the talk. Very small machines sometimes do not provide sufficiently clear audio volume. Tape decks "jacked" into home stereo units usually provide good playback.

Initially the program leaders will select the Scripture passage of five to fifteen verses that will be used in the praying phase of the meeting. As the group matures members should be encouraged to take turns in selecting the passages. The selected passage should be relevant to the study theme (i.e., develop, complement, support or clarify the theme) and appropriate for personal and group prayer. We have found Biblical Concordances and Topical Bible Indexes to be particularly useful in making these selections. Also refer to the resource list in the last chapter for books that will contribute additional enrichment background on the chosen passages. One's own prayerful reflection during the private reading and praying of various passages will probably be the primary means of discerning what passage seems appropriate for a given meeting.

STRUCTURE OF A HOME PROGRAM MEETING

The structure of a home program meeting is the basic format of *study, sharing and praying Scripture* as described in Chapter 2.

The **STUDY phase** incorporates one or more of the methods of study input described in the previous section.

The **SHARING phase** of the meeting entails group discussion of the biblical meaning of the study input, ultimately leading to individual sharing on how the material "spoke" to them personally. We suggest that each participant obtain a notebook wherein he/she keeps notes on salient points heard during the **STUDY phase** of the meeting. Each member is encouraged to "jot" down key thoughts, questions, or notes on material that brought forth a personal response, for later sharing within the group.

The *praying phase* of the meeting is mediated by using the basic scriptural praying method or one of the suggested variations as described in Chapter 2, wherein the selected passage is:

First read slowly and prayerfully to the group, followed by a few moments of silent prayerful reflection, and then personal sharing by the members within the group.

Read a second time—slowly and prayerfully, followed by silent prayerful reflection, and again by personal sharing.

Read a third time, followed by a few moments of reflection, and then prayed by each member as they are led to praise, adore, give thanks etc.

Initially about three to five minutes are allowed for each of the three readings and the subsequent sharing and praying. As the group matures the overall time is extended up to thirty or more minutes.

Each member is encouraged to assume individual responsibility for meaningful participation in the sharing and praying phases of each meeting. The leaders may need to remind new groups of the importance of individual participation, which is so necessary to the continued building of Christian community.

Providing refreshments in the form of coffee or tea during the entire meeting adds to a relaxed environment. If at any time during the **STUDY** or **SHARING phase** of a meeting a participant wishes to partake, he/she does so quietly without interrupting the rest of the group. We do not encourage getting refreshments or moving around during the praying phase of the meeting. Allowing participants to move about a little, makes even an hour long taped-talk considerably more bearable. We have restricted our refreshments to simple coffee, tea, etc., for we have found that anything more elaborate tends to disturb the tranquility of the meeting and in the long run becomes expensive.

The overall length of the meeting can be adaptable to the needs of your particular group. The one hour to one and a half hour meeting format is usually adapted for youth ministry Scripture groups, college-level (Newman Club) groups, "lunchtime" programs and early evening groups. The more frequently used two and a half hour meeting format is adaptable for daytime and nighttime home or parish programs.

Small groups always permit greater flexibility in scheduling the meetings, which may be weekly or twice monthly. We have found that monthly meetings often lose continuity, and community does not build as rapidly as in weekly or twice a month meetings. Whereas larger parish programs may have to adjourn for the summer months, the home programs can continue throughout the year, adjusting meeting dates to accommodate holidays, vacations, etc.

ROLE OF LEADERS

The leader couple (or team) of a Home Scripture Program have the general responsibility for the smooth, efficient functioning of the meetings. They are responsible for a suitable and comfortable meeting place, simple refreshments (i.e., coffee, tea, cocoa, etc.), and for adequate and appropriate equipment in the event cassettes, films, filmstrips or videotapes are to be used. The leaders preview and select suggested material for the **STUDY phase** of the program, although all members of the group should generally agree on the final selection of Scripture themes and subject matter. The leaders are also responsible for assigning to another member the responsibility for selecting the following meeting's scriptural prayer-passage.

The leader couple are an influential factor in the building-up of the spirit of Christian community within the group. Calling members after a missed meeting to communicate the next meeting-date and the assigned home reading enables participants to maintain continuity and feel wanted within the group. We have found the greatest aids to building community-spirit, outside the regular Scripture Program meetings, have been periodic group potluck dinners, special evenings simply set aside for fellowshiping, and holiday and special occasion parties. A once or twice a year home Celebration of the Eucharist can be a profound spiritual catalyst to experience awareness of the spirit of community that has grown within a Scripture Program group!

FIRST YEAR THEME DEVELOPMENT

A home group's first-year study input will usually be provided primarily by a series of taped talks.

We have found that an overview of the Old and New Testaments provides a much needed and appreciated scriptural foundation upon which further indepth studies can be developed. For many first-year program participants, a basic introduction to Scripture is necessary and beneficial before focusing indepth on a specific book of the Bible. Themes and related resources suggested for introductory first-year programs are listed later in this chapter. Some introductory Scripture themes developed by sets of taped talks are:

Great Themes of Scripture: Overview of the Old Testament, R. Rohr, O.F.M.

Great Themes of Scripture: Overview of the New Testament, R. Rohr, O.F.M.

Jesus and His Church: Overview of the New Testament, R. Rohr, O.F.M.

Enjoying the Old Testament, G. Montague

Enjoying the New Testament, G. Montague

Toward Understanding the New Testament Series, edited by L. Boadt

Following are two of the suggested themes, resources and meeting outlines for a first-year home program using taped talks as its primary study input. For use with these taped talks there are corresponding Home Reading Guides listed in the Parish Scriptures Program Chapter 4, Appendix G.

SERIES I—THEME: INTRODUCTORY OVERVIEW OF THE OLD TESTAMENT

Series' length: 9 meetings.

Resources: taped talks and books.

TAPED TALKS	BOOKS
Brotherhood, A New Way of Living: Praying Scripture (1) D. Rosage, S.J. *Great Themes of Scripture: Overview of the Old Testament* (6) R. Rohr, O.F.M.	*Reading Scripture as the Word of God* G. Martin *Speak Lord, Your Servant Is Listening!* D. Rosage, S.J. *Pathways in Scripture* D. Winzen, O.S.B. *Man Meets God* Rev. R. Humitz

Additional enrichment books are suggested at specific meetings for further development of a particular theme. However, assigned reading is given only from the basic recommended books listed above.

SUGGESTED STUDY INPUT OUTLINE:

Meeting #1 Explanation of Scripture Program Purpose and Format and Get Acquainted Time
Meeting #2 Tape, *The Call: Introduction to the Word*
Meeting #3 Tape, *Brotherhood, A New Way of Living: Praying Scripture*
Meeting #4 Tape, *Exodus: The Journey of Faith*
Meeting #5 Tape, *Joshua to Kings: Ordinary Becomes Extraordinary*
Meeting #6 Tape, *The Prophets: Radical Traditionists*
Meeting #7 Tape, *Genesis: God and Man* (first half of tape)
Meeting #8 Tape, *Job: Good and Evil* (last half of tape)
Meeting #9 Tape, *Salvation History: Faith in Evolution*

SERIES II—THEME: INTRODUCTORY OVERVIEW OF THE NEW TESTAMENT

Series' length: 7 meetings.

Resources: taped talks, books, audio-visuals.

TAPED TALKS	BOOKS	AUDIO-VISUALS
Jesus and His Church: Overview of the New Testament (6) R. Rohr, O.F.M. *Man Meets God* Rev. R. Humitz *Who Do You Say That I Am?* Rev. E. Ciuba	*Pathways In Scripture* D. Winzen, O.S.B.	*Slides of the Holy Land* Presented by program member or guest who has been there as a visitor and would like to share about his/her trip.

SUGGESTED STUDY-INPUT OUTLINE:

Meeting #1 Tape, *Matthew's Good News: The Reign of God*
Meeting #2 Tape, *Mark and John: Jesus Is Lord*
Meeting #3 Tape, *Luke and Acts: A New Life*
Meeting #4 Tape, *Mary, Prayer And The Church*
Meeting #5 Tape, *Paul: A New Life In Christ*
Meeting #6 Tape, *Apocalypse: The New Creation*
Meeting #7 Guest, *Holy Land Slide Presentation and Sharing of Trip*
Celebration of Eucharist: as Thanksgiving for Year
Concluding with Potluck Lunch (Dinner or Dessert)

A Typical Meeting

A typical Home Scripture Program meeting will begin with a prayer for God's blessing upon the time to be spent together. We usually join hands forming a circle and allow time for each one who so wishes to contribute to the prayer, and then move immediately into the study phase. The guest speaker and his/her topic, or the taped-talk, or audio-visual media is introduced and study input begun. The meeting time is dictated by the length of the input and the amount of time a group wishes to share and pray. Normally, the **STUDY phase** is forty-five minutes to an hour, the **SHARING phase** forty-five minutes and the **PRAYING phase** thirty minutes, roughly totaling two and a half hours.

The flexibility of a home program allows the talk to be interrupted, questioned or (if a tape) replayed as desired by the group. On occasions, we have interrupted a taped-talk and begun the **SHARING phase** early, finishing the remainder of the talk at a later meeting. The length of the **SHARING phase** is also flexible. We have found through experience, however, that no phase of the meeting should be "skipped" or deleted. That is, we always manage our time so that we have a meaningful **STUDY phase**, **SHARING phase**, and most especially a **PRAYING SCRIPTURE phase**. It's easy to get so involved in a good sharing that time "flies" and no time is left for praying. We have made this mistake and the entire group suffered from this mismanagement of time. Now, we always allow adequate time in each meeting for the scriptural praying.

As the meeting time comes to an end the next meeting date is determined, topic set, and home reading assigned by program leaders. Then forming a circle as hands are joined, the members conclude the meeting with a few minutes of shared spontaneous prayers of thanksgiving (for the meeting, etc.), and special concerns (individual needs, etc.). Fellowship follows the meeting as long as it is convenient for members to remain.

Alternative Study-Input Approaches and Development of Themes

As previously mentioned, a series of taped talks developing an "Overview of the Old and New Testaments" usually provides the study input for the first year of a home program. From the second year on, as the members mature in their study of Scripture, they may want to be less dependent upon taped talks and more innovative and personally involved in the preparation of the study input for the meetings.

Series themes that are easily developed by individual members through reports or teachings are: the Prophets, the Epistles, a Gospel studied by sections or chapters, the men and women of Scripture, the Sunday liturgical readings, etc. The group mutually selects the theme to be developed, along with a compatible (basic) Scripture commentary or study guide.

Taking turns, each member assumes full responsibility for the study-input for a meeting (or several meetings within the series). This should include the preparation of a report or teaching along with discussion questions relative to the content of the presentation, and the selection of a Scripture passage for group praying.

Following are three alternate approaches for the study-input of a home Scripture Program. These approaches depend primarily upon the individual member's prepared report or teaching which is presented during the meeting's **STUDY phase**.

The "reports" referred to in these three alternatives usually average ten to twenty minutes in length and are based solely on the assigned home Scripture commentary or study-guide reading. When the **SHARING phase** is to be dependent upon the assigned home reading, then reports given at the beginning of the meeting enable all the members fo join actively in the discussions, even when unexpected circumstances may have prevented some from completing their reading assignments. Reports also serve to refresh the memory of what was read prior to the meeting and thereby facilitate more involved group participation.

The "teachings" referred to in these alternatives usually average twenty to sixty minutes in length and provide additional information beyond the scope of the assigned home reading. In preparing his/her teaching, the member makes use of Scripture, commentaries, study guides and enrichment books in addition to the "basic" reading assigned to the group. Taped talks are often used as additional background information sources when preparing the teachings.

In the first alternative, the study input is totally dependent upon the participants' prepared home study and the report given by a member during the **STUDY phase** of the meeting. In the second alternative, the study input is primarily dependent upon a member's teaching. Seldom are taped talks or audio-visuals used in these first two alternate approaches to the study input. In the third alternative, the development of the theme allows for a balanced coordination of the members' reports or teachings, selected taped talks and audio-visuals for the study input. Suggested "meeting models" are also included in the third approach using various resources to develop the themes for two different length meetings.

The suggested themes and meeting timetables are only a few examples of the numerous themes available and the many ways these themes can be developed for a Scripture Program. To also assist you in developing your own unique Scripture Program series, refer to the wide listing of themes and related resources suggested later in this chapter.

ALTERNATIVE NO. 1

This approach utilizes a Scripture commentary or study guide as the primary study input in addition to readings in Scripture. All members are requested to faithfully prepare the assigned home readings. At the beginning of each meeting, a member gives a detailed report on the assigned reading. Sharing follows based on the home readings, the member's report and the discussion questions found in the book or specially prepared by the "reporting" member. The individual giving the report also selects the Scripture passage for the group Scripture prayer.

This approach to studying, sharing and praying Scripture in a small group can be among the most rewarding of all the suggested study methods. It draws each member into commitment and involvement in sharing the responsibility for a fruitful meeting. This approach is also the most demanding and time consuming in that it requires all members of the group to prepare consistently for each and every meeting. We have found that the personal circumstances of the members and the time they can give to the meeting preparation will determine to what extent this approach can be used, and for how long a period it can be viable within a given group. There is a degree of pressure in required regular personal preparation, especially if the entire studying and sharing phases of the meeting depend upon a faithful fulfilling of that commitment. Therefore, some variety can be very enriching. We've found that this approach is enhanced by an occasional taped talk, guest speaker or audio-visual aid.

Following is a list of Scripture commentaries and study guides that could be satisfactorily used as the primary study input. Most have discussion questions at the end of each chapter to facilitate group sharings.

Reading the New Testament: An Introduction, by Pheme Perkins

Man Meets God, by Rev. Robert Humitz

Scripture Discussion Commentary Series, by ACTA Foundation (12 volumes)

The Daily Study Bible Series, by William Barclay (17 volumes, no discussion questions)

Reading Scripture as the Word of God, by George Martin (no discussion questions)

Pathways in Scripture, by Rev. Damasus Winzen (no discussion questions)

Discovering the Bible, by Rev. John Tickle

These Stones Will Shout, by Rev. Mark Link (no discussion questions)

Invitation to Matthew, by Rev. Donald Senior

Invitation to Mark, by Rev. Paul Achtemeier

Invitation to Luke, by Rev. Robert Karris

Invitation to John, by Rev. George MacRae

Who Do You Say I Am? by Rev. Edward Ciuba

The Seventh Trumpet, by Rev. Mark Link (no discussion questions)

A Commentary on the Gospel of Matthew, by Rev. Albert Kirk and Rev. Robert Obach

Alive in the Spirit: The Church in the Acts of the Apostles, by Thomas Smith (separate guide-book for group leaders)

Good News About Jesus as Told by Mark, by Thomas J. Smith (separate guide-book for group leaders)

The Images of Jesus (Exploring the Metaphors in Matthew's Gospel), by Daniel O'Connor and Jacques Jimenez

ALTERNATIVE NO. 2

This study approach depends primarily upon scriptural teachings prepared and presented by members within the group. Following is an example using this approach that develops a theme on the *"Old Testament Major and Minor Prophets."* There are approximately twelve meetings in this suggested series, with one to three prophets covered at each meeting. A single teaching may include one or more prophets, especially when presenting the minor prophets. The length of the teachings also determines how many presentations (or prophets) can be given at a single meeting.

The study input includes the teachings presented by the program members, augmented by a "basic" Scripture commentary (*) and, if desired, taped talks (*) opening and closing the series. Additional enrichment books and taped talks are suggested for the members' background information and teaching preparation.

Books:
(*) Scripture—1 and 2 Chronicles and books of the Major and Minor Prophets.

(*) *The Men and the Message of the Old Testament*, by Peter Ellis, C.SS.R.
Scripture Discussion Commentaries—#3, Prophets I, and #4, Prophets II.
Old Testament Reading Guides #14 thru #21 on the Prophets.
Listen, Prophets!—The Urgent Call for Every Christian, by George Maloney, S.J.

Taped Talks:
(*) *The Prophets: Radical Traditionists*, by Richard Rohr, O.F.M.
(*) *Intercession: Old Testament Biblical Perspective*, by Patrick Crowley, SS.CC.
The Prophets: Charismatic Men (set of 6 talks), by Carroll Stuhlmueller, C.P.

Suggested Study-Input Outline:

Meeting	**#1**	Tape, *The Prophets: Radical Traditionists*
Meeting	**#2**	Teachings, *Amos and Hosea*
Meeting	**#3**	Teachings, *Isaiah I (1–39) and Micah*
Meeting	**#4**	Teachings, *Zephaniah and Jeremiah*
Meeting	**#5**	Teachings, *Nahum, Habakkuk and Ezekiel*
Meeting	**#6**	Teaching, *Deutero-Isaiah (40–55)*
Meeting	**#7**	Teachings, *Haggai, Zechariah and Trito-Isaiah (56–66)*
Meeting	**#8**	Teachings, *Obadiah and Ezra-Nehamiah*
Meeting	**#9**	Teachings, *Malachi, Deutero-Zechariah and Joel*
Meeting	**#10**	Teachings, *Books of Jonah and Daniel*
Meeting	**#11**	Teaching, *John the Baptist*
Meeting	**#12**	Tape, *Intercession: Old Testament Biblical Perspective*

The above listing was the meeting and topic schedule followed by the members of our first home Scripture Program. We had spent three months on an overview of the Old Testament, using the taped talks, "Great Themes of Scripture" by Father Rohr. After hearing his talk on "The Prophets: Radical Traditionists" we realized our common lack of knowledge on the prophets, their lives, times and messages. We mutually decided to interrupt our Scripture-overview and spend extra time studying the prophets. Each member selected two or three prophets, agreed to read the related books of Scripture, to gather additional background information about their prophet and to share their study with the rest of the group through a scheduled teaching. Teachings varied from fifteen minutes to over an hour. Besides the historical background of each prophet and his message, the members shared parallel application of the prophets' messages for the people of God today and most importantly, what the member personally found applicable for his/her own life. A passage of Scripture from the book on the prophet was used for the meeting's group Scripture prayer. This series covered a six-month period and brought profound new knowledge, personal insight and spiritual growth for each member individually and for us as a community.

ALTERNATIVE NO. 3

The primary study input for this approach is provided by a balanced presentation from a number of resources. Study inputs utilized are teachings by a guest speaker, taped talks, audio-visuals, Scripture study guides, commentaries and enrichment books, as well as the members' own reports on assigned home reading and specially prepared indepth teachings. A sample theme: "The Gospels: Four Portraits of Jesus" is used to provide two examples (Model A and Model B) of how to coordinate such a variety of resources into a series adapted to the needs and interests of a particular program membership.

Following are the basic resources used to develop this theme. Members preparing special teachings will find additional resources under the "book" and "taped talks" sections of the last chapter and the "themes and resources" section of this chapter.

Books:
Scripture—The Four Gospels, Matthew, Mark, Luke and John.

Reading the New Testament: An Introduction, by Pheme Perkins; Part IV, Chapters #10 thru #13, The Gospels: Four Portraits of Jesus.

Taped Talks:
Towards Understanding the New Testament Series, by Paulist Press
The Nature of "Gospel," by Rev. Eugene LaVerdiere, S.S.S.
The Gospel of Mark, by Rev. Eugene LaVerdiere, S.S.S.
The Gospels of Matthew and Luke, by Rev. Eugene LaVerdiere, S.S.S.
The Gospel of John, Part I, by Rev. Richard Dillon
The Gospel of John, Part II, by Rev. Richard Dillon

Filmstrips and Records/Cassettes:
Service Evangelists Filmstrip Series, by Paulist Press
Mark—Christian Kerygma, by Rev. Terence J. Keegan, O.P.
Matthew—Discipleship, by Rev. Lawrence Boadt, C.S.P.
Luke—Prayer and Social Apostolate, by Pheme Perkins
John—Spiritually and Sacraments, by Rev. Edward Malatesta, S.J.

ALTERNATIVE NO. 3, MODEL A
(Meetings are 2½ hours long)

This two-and-a-half-hour meeting schedule is patterned after our home Scripture Program development of this same theme over a ten meeting series. Individual members took the responsibility for coordinating the presentation of various study inputs, facilitating the **SHARING phases**, and selecting the Scripture passages for praying Scripture. Assigned home reading before meetings number 2, 4, 6, and 8 included the recommendation that the members try to read the entire Gospel in one sitting. At the subsequent meetings they shared what their response was to reading each Gospel in its entirety at one time.

The total utilization of the above listed resources, coupled with members' reports and special teachings, proved to be a spiritually enriching experience for our home community. After four years of being together in a home Scripture Program, we found the more personally involved each one of us was in every aspect of the program, the stronger our sense of community and the deeper our awareness of living "rooted" in God's Word.

Members' reports, special teachings, the taped talks and filmstrips averaged twenty minutes each in length, allowing for more than one study input to be given during a regular length meeting. Following is the two-and-a-half-hour meeting format and resource outline that was adapted for dual study inputs and **SHARING phases** for nine meetings. A guest speaker provided the single study input for the tenth meeting.

A Two-and-a-Half-Hour Meeting Format Using Dual Study-Inputs and Sharing Phases.

20 minutes—first **STUDY PHASE** (report, taped talk or filmstrip),

40 minutes—**SHARING phase**,

20 minutes—second **STUDY phase** (report, teaching, taped talk or filmstrip),

40 minutes—**SHARING phase**,

30 minutes—**PRAYING SCRIPTURE phase**.

Suggested Dual Study-Input Outline:

Meeting #1   Tape, *The Nature of "Gospel"*
Report, *Reading the New Testament*, Part II, Chapter 5, The Risen Christ: Beginnings of Christology

Meeting #2   Report, *Reading the New Testament*, Part IV, Chapter 10, Mark: Jesus, Hidden and Suffering Messiah
Tape, *The Gospel of Mark*

Meeting #3   Teaching, (special theme developed in Gospel of Mark)
Filmstrip, *Mark—Christian Kerygma*

Meeting #4   Report, *Reading the New Testament*, Part IV, Chapter 11, Matthew: Jesus, the True Teacher of Israel
Filmstrip, *Matthew—Discipleship*

Meeting #5   Teaching, (special theme developed in Gospel of Matthew).
Tape, *The Gospels of Matthew and Luke*

Meeting #6   Report, *Reading the New Testament*, Part IV, Chapter 12, Luke: Jesus, Son of God
Filmstrip, *Luke—Prayer and Social Apostolate*

Meeting #7   Guest Speaker, teaching on *The Infancy Narratives*.

Meeting #8   Report, *Reading the New Testament*, Part IV, Chapter 13, John: Jesus, the Divine Word
Tape, *The Gospel of John, Part I*

Meeting #9   Tape, *The Gospel of John, Part II*
Teaching, (special theme in Gospel of John).

Meeting #10   Filmstrip, *John—Spirituality and Sacraments*
(Show the filmstrip twice for deeper enrichment, with Scripture prayer after the second showing.)

ALTERNATIVE NO. 3, MODEL B
(Meetings are either one hour or one-and-one-half hours in length.)

This meeting format and resource outline is patterned after a Scripture Program adapted for a local college Newman Club group that meets weekly during their lunchtime. They were interested in an overview of the Gospels as their introduction into Bible study, but had limited time for meeting preparation. The Religious sister on campus adapted the format and resources to meet their needs and interests. She gave the reports on the suggested home reading and special teachings developing specific themes in each Gospel. She also coordinated the use of the taped talks and filmstrips, selected the Scripture passages for prayer and facilitated the group sharings and discussions. Feedback was positive and encouraging for future program themes with greater involvement by the young people.

A One Hour Meeting Format Using a Single Study Input:
20 minutes—**STUDY PHASE** (report, teaching, taped talk or filmstrip),
20 minutes—**SHARING phase**,
20 minutes—**PRAYING SCRIPTURE phase.**
OR

One and Half Hour Meeting, With a Single Study Input:
20 minutes—**STUDY phase** (report, teaching, taped talk, or audio-visual),
40 minutes—**SHARING phase**,
30 minutes—**PRAYING SCRIPTURE phase.**

Suggested Study-Input Outline:

Meeting #1   Report, *Reading the New Testament*, Part IV, Chapter 10, Mark: Jesus, Hidden and Suffering Messiah

Meeting #2   Tape, *The Gospel of Mark*

Meeting #3   Teaching, (special theme in Gospel of Mark . . .)

Meeting #4   Filmstrip, *Mark—Christian Kerygma*

Meeting #5   Report, *Reading the New Testament*, Part IV, Chapter 11, Matthew: Jesus, the True Teacher of Israel

Meeting #6   Teaching, (special theme in Gospel of Matthew . . .)

Meeting #7   Filmstrip, *Matthew—Discipleship*

Meeting #8   Tape, *The Gospels of Matthew and Luke*

Meeting #9   Report, *Reading the New Testament*, Part IV, Chapter 12, Luke: Jesus, Son of God

Meeting #10 Teaching, (special theme in Gospel of Luke . . .)

Meeting #11 Filmstrip, *Luke—Prayer and Social Apostolate*

Meeting #12 Report, *Reading the New Testament*, Part IV, Chapter 13, John: Jesus, the Divine Word

Meeting #13 Tape, *The Gospel of John, Part I*

Meeting #14 Tape, *The Gospel of John, Part II*

Meeting #15 Teaching, (special theme in Gospel of John . . .)

Meeting #16 Filmstrip, *John—Spirituality and Sacraments*

SUGGESTED THEMES AND RELATED RESOURCES FOR SUBSEQUENT YEARS

The abundance of scriptural resources makes possible numerous options in the selection and development of Scripture Program themes. The availability of a regular speaker or occasional guest speakers will add unlimited potential to theme choices and ways of using compatible resources over a series of meetings. Program leaders should dare to be creative and flexible in selecting and interchanging the suggested resources for a particular theme, whether the primary study input is by speaker, video-tapes or taped talks.

Speakers, regular or guest, can use these same study aids to augment their presentations. Taped talks picked out of a series or singular in nature can add variety and highlight specific aspects of the theme being developed by a regular speaker. The flexibility of having several taped talks to select from in case of the speaker's unexpected cancellation or simply to add variety to the study input is a definite asset in coordinating Scripture Programs.

Following are thirty-three proposed biblical themes that can be developed into various length series with selected taped talks, books, audio-visuals and video-tapes. Contained within these suggested themes are over sixty-two sets of taped talks, a hundred books, several dozen films and filmstrips and twelve sets of video-tapes. Refer to the last chapter for complete address information on all the suggested resources.

Taped talks are listed by sets (the number of talks in each set is stated in parentheses) that can be used as the primary study input when no regular speaker is available. The majority of taped talks are forty-five to sixty minutes in length. The longer tapes are best suited for programs where the meetings are two to two and a half hours in length. However, the shorter length tapes can also be used effectively in the longer meetings that allow for an hour study input in the following ways: (a) one taped talk with extended sharing time; (b) two taped talks played in tandem when the subject matter is compatible, followed by the **SHARING phase**; (c) showing of an audio-visual that complements the subject matter of the taped talk, which is then played and followed by the usual **SHARING phase**. The length of a series is dictated by the number of taped talks in a set, the length of the talks and/or the number used at a meeting and the number of audio-visuals used per series. The additional enrichment taped talks and audio-visuals that are listed for each theme can be added or substituted within the "basic" set for a series. Many of the audio-visuals and books suggested for a certain theme are equally compatible with several other themes.

What we are suggesting is that a certain tape doesn't necessarily have to be used only with a certain book or audio-visual! However, *when we've found that certain books and audio visuals are more compatible and supportive of the theme development with a particular tape, we've arranged them horizontally and marked them with an asterisk (*).* But always, program leaders should listen, read and observe each resource for themselves; coordinating the materials that seem best suited for the needs and interests of their program membership!

Once you become familiar with the variety of available resources, your own creativity, ingenuity and flexibility can lead to the development of the "perfect" program for your first-year home or parish group. Rather than feeling overwhelmed with all the suggested titles of books, tapes and A-Vs, our aim is to enable people to discover the fantastic "storehouse" out of which we can select and bring forth the "best" of solid Catholic biblical resources for our people.

Your choice of tapes, books and audio-visuals to augment and enrich the chosen theme and how each is used within the program format will make your Scripture Program totally unique and most serviceable for your participants. No two home or parish programs are exactly alike!

THEME: INTRODUCTION TO SCRIPTURE I—STUDY AND SHARING

Suggested use: study aid for use at one or more introductory meetings of a series.
Resources: speakers, taped talks, books and audio-visuals.

TAPED TALKS	BOOKS	AUDIO-VISUALS
The Call: Introduction to the Word, R. Rohr (1)	*Reading Scripture as the Word of God*, G. Martin *The Bible and You*, A Scriptographic Booklet	*Literary Forms: A Key to Understand the Bible
Alternate Sets God's Revelation in the Bible, J. Reese and What Is Biblical "Inspiration"? J. Reese	The New Guide to Reading and Studying the Bible, W. Harrington	

Additional Enrichment Study Input

The Nature of "Gospel," E. LaVerdiere Free to Witness, M. Link (1) Scripture is Credible/ Professional Dynamic, M. Link (1)	Divine Revelation, Vatican II Documents Evangelization in the Modern World, Pope Paul VI Reading the Bible: A Guide to the Word of God for Everyone, J. K. Dalpadado	Jerusalem, 66 A.D., Geography of the Holy Land Archaeology and the Living New Testament

31

THEME: INTRODUCTION TO SCRIPTURE II—PRAYING SCRIPTURE

Suggested use: study aids for use at one introductory meeting of a series.
Resources: speakers, taped talks and books.

TAPED TALKS	BOOKS
*Brotherhood; A New Way of Living: Praying Scripture (1), D. Rosage	*Speak Lord, Your Servant Is Listening, D. Rosage

Additional Enrichment Prayer Guides

Praying and Living with Scriptures, (1), R. Tichenor Praying with the Scriptures (1), E. LaVerdiere Biblical Prayer (1), J. Walsh Praying the Psalms (1), T. Dubay Communical Prayer in a Biblical Spirit (1), T. Dubay	Discovering Pathways in Prayer, D. Rosage Trumpets of Beaten Metal: Biblical Prayer, E. LaVerdiere Biblical Prayer, E. Lussier Pray—An Introduction to the Spiritual Life for Busy People, R. Huelsman The Spirit Speaks in Us—Biblical Way of Praying, J. Sheets Face to Face with God—The Bible's Way of Praying, J. Loew

THEME: OVERVIEW OF THE OLD TESTAMENT (INTRODUCTORY FIRST-YEAR PROGRAM #1)

Series' length: 6–8 meetings.
Resources: speakers, taped talks, books and audio-visuals.

TAPED TALKS	BOOKS	AUDIO-VISUALS
*Great Themes of Scripture: Over-view of the Old Testament (6), R. Rohr	*Man Meets God, R. Humitz Pathways in Scripture, D. Winzen	*Exodus of Israel *Exodus of Jesus
Additional Enrichment Study Input		
Enjoying the Old Testament (4), G. Montague Intercession—Old Testament Biblical Perspective (1), P. Crowley	The Men and the Message of the Old Testament, P. Ellis These Stones Will Shout, M. Link The Threshing Floor, J. Sheehan The Psalms, J. Fischer Discovering the Biblical World, H. Frank	The Exodus The Passover Nomad Life of the Hebrews Religious Life of the Hebrews

THEME: OVERVIEW OF THE NEW TESTAMENT (INTRODUCTORY FIRST-YEAR PROGRAM #2)

Series' length: 6–10 meetings.
Resources: speakers, taped talks, books and audio-visuals.

TAPED TALKS	BOOKS	AUDIO-VISUALS
*Jesus and His Church: Overview of the New Testament (6), R. Rohr Alternate Set Great Themes of Scripture: Overview of the New Testament (6), R. Rohr	*Who Do You Say That I Am? E. Ciuba *Pathways in Scripture, D. Winzen	*Gospel According to Matthew *Gospel According to Mark *Gospel According to Luke *Gospel According to John

Additional Enrichment Study Input

Enjoying the New Testament (4), G. Montague Understanding the Gospels (5), G. Montague Suffering to Glory: Passion Narratives and Resurrection Appearances (2), E. LaVerdiere	The Seventh Trumpet, M. Link Daily Life in the Time of Jesus, H. Daniel-Rops Jesus, A. D. Sertillanges Scripture for Meditation Series: The Passion, H. Wansbrough The Resurrection, H. Wansbrough Building Christ's Body, G. Montague The Humor of Jesus, H. Cormier Discovering the Biblical World, H. Frank	The Geography of the Holy Land Archaeology and the Living New Testament Where Jesus Lived The Parable

THEME: OVERVIEW OF THE NEW TESTAMENT (INTRODUCTORY FIRST-YEAR PROGRAM #3)

Series' length: 9–18 meetings.
Resources: speakers, taped talks, books and audio-visuals.

TAPED TALKS

*Toward Understanding the New Testament Series (18), Edited by L. Boadt

BOOKS

*Reading the New Testament, P. Perkins

AUDIO-VISUALS

*Matthew—Discipleship, L. Boadt
*Mark—Christian Kerygma, T. Keegan
*Luke—Prayer and Social Apostolate, P. Perkins
*John—Spirituality and Sacrament, E. Malatesta

THEME: MEETING CHRIST IN THE SYNOPTIC GOSPELS (INTRODUCTORY FIRST-YEAR PROGRAM #4)

Series' length: 14 meetings.
Resources: speakers, single taped talks, books and audio-visuals.

TAPED TALKS	BOOKS	AUDIO-VISUALS
(Combination of single talks and talks excerpted from tape sets.) *The Nature of "Gospel," E. LaVerdiere *Matthew's Good News: The Reign of God, R. Rohr *Christian Living and the Beatitudes, P. Crowley *Christ's Healing Ministry in the Gospels, P. Crowley *"Do This In Remembrance of Me," E. LaVerdiere *The Gospel of Mark, E. LaVerdiere *Mark and John: Jesus Is Lord, R. Rohr *Mark: Following the Suffering Messiah, E. LaVerdiere *The Gospels of Matthew and Luke, E. LaVerdiere *The Poor Church in Luke's Gospel, R. Karris *The Way to Emmaus: Luke 24:13–35, E. LaVerdiere *Luke and Acts: A New Life, R. Rohr *Jesus Christ: Model Intercessor, R. Tichenor	*Reading the New Testament, P. Perkins *Who Do You Say That I Am?, E. Ciuba	*Who Is Jesus? P. Perkins *Matthew—Discipleship, L. Boadt *Mark—Christian Kerygma, T. Keegan *Luke—Prayer and Social Apostolate, P. Perkins *The Parable
	Additional Enrichment Study Input	
	The Key to the Good News—Jesus Christ Is Lord! G. Kosicki Jesus, Lord and Christ, J. O'Grady Jesus, A. D. Sertillanges Meeting Jesus—A New Way to Christ, L. Santucci Bright Darkness—Jesus Christ, G. Maloney The Images of Jesus, D. O'Connor and J. Jimenez The Humor of Jesus, H. Cormier Nesting in the Rock—Jesus, the Way to the Father, G. Maloney Praying with Scripture in the Holy Land, Msgr. D. Rosage Scripture for Meditation Series: Our Divine Master The Conspiracy of God: The Holy Spirit in Us, J. Haughey Parables Told by Jesus, W. Harrington	The Great Mystique Shatterer (for prayer) Bread and Wine (for prayer) Gifts and Talents (for prayer)

THEME: THE PROPHETS

Series' length: 6–10 meetings.
Resources: speakers, taped talks, books and audio-visuals.

TAPED TALKS	BOOKS	AUDIO-VISUALS
The Prophets: Charismatic Men (6), C. Stuhlmueller Alternate Sets *Prophet Isaiah* (7), J. Wolfe or *Old Testament Prophecy* (10), G. Montague	*The Men and the Message of the Old Testament*, P. Ellis *Old Testament Reading Guide #20, Isaiah 40–66*, C. Stuhlmueller *Scripture Discussion Commentaries #3, Prophets I #4, Prophets II	
Additional Enrichment Study Input		
The Prophets: Radical Traditionists (1), R. Rohr *Intercession: Old Testament Biblical Perspective* (1), P. Crowley	*Listen, Prophets!* G. Maloney Old Testament Reading Guides: #14, *Introduction to the Prophetical Books of O.T.*, B. Vawter #15, *Amos, Hosea, Micah*, N. Flanagan #16, *Isaiah 1–39*, M. McNamara #17, *Jeremiah, Baruch*, C. Stuhlmueller #18, *Ezekiel*, J. Turro #19, *Zephaniah, Nahum, Habakkuk, Lamentations, Obadiah*, G. Montague #21, *Haggai, Zechariah, Malachi, Joel*, G. Denzer	*Out of Darkness* (for prayer) *Witness* (for prayer) *They Shall See* (for prayer) *Psalm 23* (for prayer)

THEME: THE PENTATEUCH

Series' length: 10–15 meetings.
Resources: speakers, taped talks, books and audio-visuals.

TAPED TALKS	BOOKS	AUDIO-VISUALS
*Genesis and Exodus (10), F. Montalbano	*Old Testament Reading Guides: #2, Exodus, M. Bourke #4, Genesis 12–50, R. Faley #9, Genesis 1–11, W. Heidt	*The Exodus *Nomad Life of the Hebrews *Religious Life of the Hebrews
Additional Enrichment Study Input		
Exodus: Journey of Faith (1), R. Rohr Genesis: God and Man (1), R. Rohr Salvation History: Faith in Evolution (1), R. Rohr Intercession: Old Testament Biblical Perspective (1), P. Crowley	The Men and the Message of the Old Testament, P. Ellis Scripture Discussion Commentary #1, Pentateuch The Threshing Floor, J. Sheehan Let the People Cry Amen, J. Sheehan These Stones Will Shout, M. Link Scripture for Meditation Series: Christian Deuteronomy Discovering the Biblical World, H. Frank	The Passover Exodus of Israel Exodus of Jesus Song for the Universe (for prayer) Come to Life (for prayer) Buttercup (for prayer)

THEME: THE PSALMS

Series' length: 6–10 meetings.
Resources: speakers, taped talks, books and audio-visuals.

TAPED TALKS	BOOKS	AUDIO-VISUALS
The Psalms: A School of Prayer (6), R. Murphy **Alternate Set** **The Psalms* (10), G. Montague	**Out Of The Depths*, Bernhard Anderson **The Psalms Are Our Prayers*, A. Gelin *Old Testament Reading Guide #23, The Psalms*, R. MacKenzie	
Additional Enrichment Study Input		
Praying the Psalms (1), T. Dubay *The Psalms: Israel's Prayer* (1), R. Murphy	*Praying the Psalms*, K. Stradling *A Shepherd Looks At Psalm 23*, Phillip Keller *Scripture Discussion Commentary #6, Wisdom*, ACTA *The Psalms, Job*, R. Murphy *Praying the Psalms*, T. Merton	*Song for the Universe* (for prayer) *Psalm 23* (for prayer) *Images 1:5—for A Surfer, Psalm 139* (for prayer)

THEME: GOSPEL OF MATTHEW

Series' length: 5–10 meetings.
Resources: speakers, taped talks, books and audio-visuals.

TAPED TALKS	BOOKS	AUDIO-VISUALS
*Gospel of Matthew (8), J. Grassi **Alternate Set** Gospel of Matthew (5), G. Montague	*A Commentary on the Gospel of Matthew, A. Kirk and R. Obach *Invitation to Matthew: A Commentary, D. Senior *Read and Pray: Gospel of St. Matthew, D. Senior	*Matthew—Discipleship, L. Boadt *Reconciliation in the Gospel of Matthew, J. Reese

Additional Enrichment Study Input

Matthew's Good News: The Reign of The Gospels of Matthew and Luke (1), E. LaVerdiere Christian Living and the Beatitudes (1), P. Crowley Christ's Healing Ministry (1), P. Crowley	Man Meets God, R. Humitz The Kingdom and the Glory, A. McBride New Testament Reading Guide: #4, Gospel of Matthew, D. Stanley Scripture Discussion Commentary #7, Mark and Matthew The Daily Study Bible Series: The Gospel of Matthew, Vol. I & II, W. Barclay Parables of Jesus, E. Flood A Key to the Parables, W. Harrington Healing: Reflections on the Gospel, G. Martin Scripture for Meditation Series: Infancy Narratives, J. Bligh Parables Told by Jesus, W. Harrington The Images of Jesus, D. O'Connor and J. Jimenez The Humor of Jesus, H. Cormier	The Gospel According to St. Matthew (2 hour film) The Parable Sermon on the Mount The Beatitude Series: (for prayer) They Shall See Those Who Mourn Theirs is the Kingdom Matthew 5:5

THEME: THE GOSPEL OF MARK

Series' length: 10–22 meetings.
Resources: speakers, taped talks, books and audio-visuals.

TAPED TALKS	BOOKS	AUDIO-VISUALS
Gospel of Mark (20), D. Senior **Alternate Sets** *Gospel of Mark* (10), J. Grassi or *Gospel of Mark* (22), J. O'Bryne or *Gospel of Mark* (10), R. Rohr	**Invitation to Mark*, P. Achtemeier **Read & Pray: Gospel of St. Mark*, P. Van Linden **New Testament Reading Guide: #2, Gospel of Mark*, G. Sloyan **Scripture Discussion Commentary #7, Mark and Matthew*	**Mark—Christian Kerygma*, T. Keegan **Faith in the Gospel of Mark*, S. Freyne **The Gospel According to Mark*

Additional Enrichment Study Input

Mark: Following the Suffering Messiah (1), E. LaVerdiere *Gospel of Mark* (1), E. LaVerdiere *Mark and John: Jesus Is Lord* (1), R. Rohr	*The Mustard Seed*, M. Link *The Daily Study Bible Series: The Gospel of Mark*, W. Barclay *Jesus Alive! The Mighty Message of Mark*, T. J. Smith *Good News About Jesus as Told by Mark*, T. J. Smith *Parables Told by Jesus*, W. J. Harrington *The Humor of Jesus*, H. Cormier	*The Parable* *It's About This Carpenter* (for prayer) *The Great Mystique Shatterer* (for prayer)

THEME: THE GOSPEL OF LUKE

Series' length: 10 meetings.
Resources: speakers, taped talks, books and audio-visuals.

TAPED TALKS	BOOKS	AUDIO-VISUALS
Gospel of Luke (10), J. Grassi Alternate Sets *Gospel of Luke* (10), R. Rohr	**Invitation to Luke*, R. Karris **Read and Pray: Gospel of St. Luke*, R. Karris	**Luke—Prayer and Social Apostolate*, P. Perkins **Prayer of Jesus in the Gospel of Luke*, T. Keegan **The Gospel According to Mark*

Additional Enrichment Study Input

The Gospel of Matthew and Luke (1), E. LaVerdiere *The Poor Church in Luke's Gospel* (1), R. Karris *The Way to Emmaus: Luke 24:13–35* (1), E. LaVerdiere *Luke and Acts: A New Life* (1), R. Rohr	*New Testament Reading Guide: #3, Gospel of Luke*, C. Stuhlmueller *Scripture Discussion Commentary #8, Luke* *The Daily Study Bible Series: The Gospel of Luke*, W. Barclay *Parables of Jesus*, E. Flood *A Key to the Parables*, W. Harrington *Meditations—A Spiritual Journey Through the Parables*, A. Bloom *Healing—Reflections on the Gospel*, G. Martin *Nesting in the Rock—Jesus the Way to the Father*, G. Maloney *Scripture for Meditation Series: Infancy Narratives*, J. Bligh *The Incarnation*, H. Wansbrough *Parables Told by Jesus*, W. J. Harrington *The Humor of Jesus*, H. Cormier	*The Greatest Dinner Party* *The Parable* *Parable of the Good Samaritan* (for prayer) *Gifts and Talents* (for prayer) *Theirs Is the Kingdom* (for prayer) *Buttercup* (for prayer)

THEME: THE GOSPEL OF JOHN

Series' length: 10–22 meetings.
Resources: speakers, taped talks, books and audio-visuals.

TAPED TALKS	BOOKS	AUDIO-VISUALS
*Gospel of St. John (10), R. Rohr **Alternate Sets** Gospel of John (24), S. Doyle or Gospel of John (10), J. Grassi or Gospel of John (22), J. O'Bryne	*New Testament Reading Guide: #13, Gospel of John, R. Brown *Invitation to John, G. MacRae *Read and Pray: Gospel of St. John, P. Perkins The Gospel of John, P. Perkins	*John—Spirituality and Sacrament, E. Malatesta *Eucharist in John's Gospel, M. Hellwig *Gospel According to John
Additional Enrichment Study Input		
The Gospel of John, Part I (1), R. Dillon The Gospel of John, Part II and the Johannine Letters (1), R. Dillon Mark and John: Jesus Is Lord (1), R. Rohr Jesus Christ: Model Intercessor (1), R. Tichenor	The Daily Study Bible Series: The Gospel of John, Vol. I & II, W. Barclay Scripture Discussion Commentary #9, John Maranatha, W. Fulco The Miracles of Jesus, H. J. Richards Woman at the Well, A. Van Kaam Looking for Jesus, A. Van Kaam The Humor of Jesus, H. Cormier Biblical Spirituality of St. John, P. de la Croix The Conspiracy of God: The Holy Spirit In Us, J. Haughey	The Parable That Kind of Love (for prayer) Right Here, Right Now (for prayer)
"Mary and Scripture" Enrichment Study Input and Prayer Guides		
TAPED TALKS	BOOKS	AUDIO-VISUALS
Mary, Prayer and the Church (1), R. Rohr Mary Revealed Through Scripture (1), J. O'Byrne	Mary—The Womb of God, G. Maloney The Glory of Israel: Scriptural Background on the Mysteries of the Rosary, R. Walls Scriptural Rosary: A modern version of the way the rosary was once prayed throughout Western Europe in the late Middle Ages.	Mary (filmstrip series), Teleketics: Woman of Faith: Mary in the Gospels Our Own Lady: Mary in the lives of her people.

THEME: THE ACTS OF THE APOSTLES

Series' length: 5–12 meetings.
Resources: speakers, taped talks, books and audio-visuals.

TAPED TALKS	BOOKS	AUDIO-VISUALS
*Acts of the Apostles (10), R. Rohr **Alternate Set** Acts of the Apostles (5), F. Montalbano	*New Testament Reading Guide #5, Acts of the Apostles, N. Flanagan *Alive in the Spirit: The Church in the Acts of the Apostles, T. Smith *Building Christ's Body: Dynamics of Christian Living According to St. Paul, G. Montague	*Community in the Acts of the Apostles, R. Rohr *The Conversion
	Additional Enrichment Study Input	
Koinonia: Life in the Early Christian Community (1), E. LaVerdiere Luke and Acts: A New Life (1), R. Rohr The Early Christian Community in Acts 1–9 (1), J. Reese St. Paul's Life and Ministry in Acts 12–28 (1), T. Keegan Paul: A Life in Christ (1), R. Rohr	Reading the New Testament: An Introduction (Part V), P. Perkins The Gospel of the Holy Spirit: A Commentary on the Acts of the Apostles, A. McBride The Daily Study Bible Series: The Acts of the Apostles, W. Barclay The Holy Spirit—Growth of a Biblical Tradition, G. Montague Scripture for Meditation Series: The Holy Spirit, H. Wansbrough The Conspiracy of God: The Holy Spirit In Us, J. Haughey A New Pentecost? L. Suenens	Many Different Gifts Pentecost (for prayer) Spirit (for prayer) Works of Faith (for prayer) Encounter (for prayer)

THEME: ST. PAUL'S LIFE AND LETTERS (INTRODUCTORY OVERVIEW)

Series' length: 5–8 meetings.
Resources: speakers, taped talks, books and audio-visuals.

TAPED TALKS	BOOKS	AUDIO-VISUALS
Paul: The Proclaimer (5), E. LaVerdiere **Alternate Sets** *Themes in Paul* (5), R. Sargent or *Life and Journeys of Paul* (3), J. O'Bryne	*Reading the New Testament: An Introduction* (Part III), P. Perkins *Building Christ's Body*, G. Montague	*The Conversion*

Additional Enrichment Study Input

Paul: A Life in Christ (1), R. Rohr *Paul: A Christian Odyssey* (1), E. LaVerdiere *St. Paul's Life and Ministry in Acts 12–28* (1), T. Keegan *St. Paul's Epistles to the Galatians and Romans* (1) T. Keegan *The Epistle to the Philippians* (1), J. Turro *The Pastoral Epistles to Timothy and Titus* (1), J. Turro	*Jesus Is Lord: Paul's Life in Christ*, J. Blenkinsopp *The Daily Study Bible Series: The Acts of the Apostles*, W. Barclay *New Testament Reading Guides:* #5, *Acts of the Apostles*, N. Flanagan #6, *Introduction to the Pauline Epistles*, B. Vawter #7, *Epistles to the Galatians and Romans*, B. Ahern #8, *First and Second Corinthians*, C. Peifer #9, *Philippians, Ephesians, Colossians, Philemon*, K. Sullivan #10, *St. Paul's Pastoral Epistles*, R. Siebeneck	*Many Different Gifts* *It's About This Carpenter* (for prayer)

THEME: GALATIANS

Series' length: 10 meetings.
Resources: speakers, taped talks and books.

TAPED TALKS	BOOKS

*Life and Journeys of Paul (3)
    J. O'Bryne
         and
*Epistle to Galatians (7),
    J. O'Bryne
	*New Testament Reading Guide #7,
	    Epistle to Galatians and
	    Romans, B. Ahern

Additional Enrichment Study Input

St. Paul's Epistles to the
    Galatians and the Romans (1),
    T. Keegan
	Scripture Discussion Commentary
	    #10, Paul I
	The Daily Study Bible Series: The
	    Letters to the Galatians and
	    Ephesians, W. Barclay

THEME: EPHESIANS AND COLOSSIANS

Series' length: 7–10 meetings.
Resources: speakers, taped talks and books.

TAPED TALKS	BOOKS

*Ephesians and Colossians (10),
    R. Sargent
 	
Alternate Set
Ephesians (7), J. Wolfe
	*New Testament Reading Guide #9,
	    Philippians, Ephesians,
	    Colossians, Philemon, K. Sullivan
	*Scripture Discussion Commentaries
	    #10, Paul I
	    #11, Paul II
	*Scripture for Meditation Series:
	    Colossians

Additional Enrichment Study Input

The Epistles to the Colossians and
    Ephesians (1), J. Turro
	The Daily Study Bible Series: The
	    Letters to the Galatians and
	    Ephesians, W. Barclay
	The Letters to the Philippians,
	    Colossians, and Thessalonians,
	    W. Barclay

THEME: CORINTHIANS

Series' length: 10 meetings.
Resources: speakers, taped talks, books and audio-visuals.

TAPED TALKS	BOOKS	AUDIO-VISUALS
*Corinthians (10), G. Montague Alternate Sets Epistle to First Corinthians (9), J. O'Bryne or Epistle to Second Corinthians (10), J. O'Bryne	*Building Christ's Body: Dynamics of Christian Living According to St. Paul, G. Montague *New Testament Reading Guide #8, First and Second Corinthians, C. Peifer	
St. Paul's First Letter to the Corinthians (1), T. Keegan Paul: A Christian Odyssey (1), E. LaVerdiere Paul: A Life in Christ (1), R. Rohr	Scripture Discussion Commentary #11, Paul II The Daily Study Bible Series: The Letters to the Corinthians, W. Barclay	Many Different Gifts Works of Faith (for prayer)

THEME: REVELATIONS

Series' Length: 7–10 meetings.
Resources: speakers, taped talks, books and audio-visuals.

TAPED TALKS	BOOKS	AUDIO-VISUALS
*The Book of Revelation (16), S. Doyle **Alternate Sets** Books of Revelation (10), F. Montalbano or Revelation (7), J. Wolfe	*New Testament Reading Guide #14, The Book of the Apocalypse, W. Heidt *Scripture Discussion Commentary #12, The Last Writings	

Additional Enrichment Study Input

The Book of Revelation (1), L. Boadt Apocalypse: The New Creation (1), R. Rohr	The Daily Study Bible Series: Revelation, Vol. I and II, W. Barclay The Book of Revelation, What Does It Really Say? J. Randall What Did Jesus Teach About the End of the World? F. Mussner	Song for the Universe (for prayer) Come to Life (for prayer) Search (for prayer) Eucharist (for prayer)

VIDEO-TAPE PRESENTATIONS

Video-tapes are adaptable for use in a home program, using the family T.V. with a video-tape deck. In a parish program they can be used with either the large screen T.V. with video-tape deck or through the diocesan cable instructional T.V. with parish T.V. outlets. For suggested resources to use with video-tapes, refer to the listings of the same theme within this section.

THEME: THE PENTATEUCH

Series' length: 10 meetings.
Resources: video-tapes and books.

VIDEO-TAPES	BOOKS
Genesis and Exodus (10), F. Montalbano	*Old Testament Reading Guides: #2 *Exodus*, M. Bourke #4 *Genesis 12–50*, R. Faley #9 *Genesis 1–110*, W. Heidt

THEME: THE PSALMS

Series' length: 10 meetings.
Resources: video-tapes and books.

VIDEO-TAPES	BOOKS
The Psalms (10), G. Montague	*Old Testament Reading Guide #23, *The Psalms*, R. MacKenzie

THEME: THE GOSPEL OF LUKE

Series' length: 10 meetings.
Resources: video-tapes and books

VIDEO-TAPES	BOOKS
Gospel of Luke (10), R. Rohr	*New Testament Reading Guide #3, *Gospel of Luke*, C. Stuhlmueller

THEME: THE ACTS OF THE APOSTLES

Series' length: 10 meetings.
Resources: video-tapes and books.

VIDEO-TAPES	BOOKS
*Acts of the Apostles (10), R. Rohr	*New Testament Reading Guide #5, Acts of the Apostles, N. Flanagan

THEME: CORINTHIANS

Series' length: 10 meetings.
Resources: video-tapes and books.

VIDEO-TAPES	BOOKS
*Corinthians (10), G. Montague	*New Testament Reading Guide #8, First and Second Corinthians, C. Peifer

THEME: EPHESIANS AND COLOSSIANS

Series' length: 10 meetings.
Resources: video-tapes and books.

VIDEO-TAPES	BOOKS
*Ephesians and Colossians (10), R. Sargent	*New Testament Reading Guide #9, Philippians, Ephesians, Colossians, Philemon, K. Sullivan

Chapter 4
PARISH SCRIPTURE PROGRAMS

AS AN OUTGROWTH OF HOME PROGRAMS

One of the real values of beginning small and building a core group of dedicated friends is the strength and experience that this community can provide in organizing and setting up parish size Scripture Programs. Most parish programs develop from home groups. It takes time for these small home groups to develop; often up to a year or more for people studying God's Word, sharing their faith-experiences and praying Scripture together to become a faith-filled, trusting community. With the experience and confidence gained, they can move into the larger parish community to establish a Scripture Program for others. One or two dedicated persons cannot coordinate and lead a parish size program. The leaders must be assisted by the love and help of a supporting community, which can "divide the work and multiply the joy."

Experience gained in a home Scripture Program is directly applicable to the parish level program. The parish program format is the same, having the study, sharing and praying phase in each meeting. Program size may initially average from thirty to more than a hundred participants, meeting regularly in the parish hall or lounge. The parish program requires a leader-couple or leader-team (of two) as well as a support group comprised of discussion leader-teams and job-coordinators who assist with the many supporting activities. Participants study, share and pray together in small table groupings of from eight to ten members.

HOW TO ORGANIZE AND SET UP A PARISH SCRIPTURE PROGRAM

A well-organized approach in the initial stages of a program will usually be rewarded later with smoother running meetings and a minimum of difficulties. Following are a few steps that we consider necessary prior to starting a parish Scripture Program.

Planning the Program
A parish level Scripture Program requires considerably more planning and organization than a home program. A sociologist once stated that when beginning a new endeavor, people always tend to underestimate others' resistance to change. Over the years experiences in implementing new programs have borne out the truth of this statement. A way to lessen the "normal" resistance to change is to set up a well thought-out detailed plan that clearly outlines all aspects of the new endeavor, especially areas of anticipated problems or difficulties. We used this technique in setting up our first parish program. The attendance and response of seventy-two parishioners at the first meeting proved the effectiveness of such preparatory efforts.

When we began thinking about how to approach our pastor regarding a parish Scripture Program it was in the late spring near the end of the first year of our home program. After developing a "briefing-type" outline of the proposed program, we presented it to our pastor for his review and consideration. We did not request a decision immediately, but left it with him for consideration, requesting an answer at a later date. The outline explained the program format, briefly described how each of the study, share and praying phases of the program would be structured, volunteered that we would be willing to be the program leader-couple and outlined our responsibilities and those of our support group. We also covered the suggested theme and study resources for the first year, proposed parish meeting dates and time, and a ninety day implementation schedule. Our implementation plan scheduled an explanation and three organizational meetings as well as certain publicity activities prior to the actual parish Scripture Program starting date. Two weeks later we were given the "go-ahead!"

The approval and support of the pastor are absolutely mandatory for the successful development of a parish Scripture Program.

Contacting Discussion Leaders
In a parish size Scripture Program the sharing-groups should be maintained between eight to ten members to insure that each member has a chance to meaningfully participate in the discussions. Each group is led by a discussion leader-couple or team (of two) who share the responsibility for their small sharing-group throughout the entire meeting.

The program leaders should solicit, through personal contact, the prospective group discussion leaders from the many persons in their parish who have group-dynamics experience and who might be interested in helping establish a parish Scripture Program. Look to parishioners with background involvement in Christian Family Movement (C.F.M.), Cursillo, Marriage-Encounter, Charismatic Renewal, teaching in Religious Education Programs, Youth Encounter Spirit and Youth Ministry or adult discussion groups for possible group-dynamics experience. Such group-dynamics experience will have provided these people with a working knowledge of how to participate and facilitate sharing in small group situations. The program leader's one-to-one contact should include a brief explanation of the program and an invitation to a general explanation meeting. A personal letter from the pastor, inviting prospective discussion leaders to the general meeting can be most helpful.

PREPARATION AND ORGANIZATIONAL MEETINGS

Meeting No. 1
General Explanation
The purpose, format and organization of a parish Scripture Program should be presented by the program leaders at the first general meeting. No commitments are requested at that meeting. Those interested in helping establish a Scripture Program in their parish as either discussion leaders or supporting job coordinators are given a questionnaire-commitment form (see Appendix A to this chapter). Within the following two weeks they are asked to prayerfully consider such a commitment in light of their present responsibilities. Only after such reflection are they requested to make their decision known (R.S.V.P.) by mailing the questionnaire-commitment form to the program leaders. Such personal commitments have been found to be quite dependable and responsible.

Following the R.S.V.P., one-on-one coordination should be conducted to assign and confirm responsibility for the various supporting jobs and ministries outlined in the Appendix C to this chapter. The more the participants can be drawn into supporting activities the more involved and committed they will be to the program. Well-coordinated assignments can significantly lessen the burden on the program leaders and insure a smoother functioning Scripture Program, so that everyone's focus of attention can be on the study, sharing and praying of God's Word within their sharing groups.

Meeting No. 2
Program Organization
The group discussion leaders and each of the job and ministry coordinators are introduced at the beginning of the organizational meeting. The second meeting should be dedicated to distributing and giving further explanation to the *"Scripture Program Job/Ministry Coordinator's Responsibilities"* (see Appendix C) as well as the *"Scripture Program Discussion Leader-Facilitator's Responsibilities"* (Appendix B). Particular emphasis should also be given to the discussion leader-facilitator's awareness of

(a) guidelines for facilitating discussion (Appendix B),

(b) concern for their table-community (Appendix B),

(c) discussion leaders' personal preparation (Appendix B).

The importance of the discussion leaders' and coordinators' adaptability, flexibility and good humor should be highlighted. Finally each group discussion leader-team is asked to select a biblical name for their table group and be prepared to share the reason for their choice with their table group at the first parish meeting.

Meeting No. 3
Communication Skills Workshop
A third meeting, a Communication Skills Workshop, should be arranged to amplify the dynamics of group sharing and to build-up the (table) discussion leaders' self-confidence. Topics that should be covered by both teaching and group-exercises include: characteristics of a good listener, a listening scale for self evaluation, discussion techniques and general points for handling problem situations. Information about the availability of trained instructors in communication skills can usually be obtained through your diocesan adult religious education office or local Catholic universities.

Our first parish Scripture Program implementation plan did not include a Communication Skills Workshop. During the setting up of subsequent programs we included the workshop in our plans. The response was most rewarding and the additional self-confidence gained by the table-discussion leaders was extremely valuable.

An excellent method of presenting the workshop is to arrange an all-day (10 A.M. to 4 P.M.) multi-parish area session. Such a workshop provides adequate time for teaching various areas of communication and facilitation, as well as an opportunity for the participants to experience the dynamics of group sharing. An all day area workshop can service many neighboring home and parish Scripture Programs and can be open to attendance by both discussion leaders and other interested participants. When an area has a number of ongoing home and parish Scripture Programs, as well as newly developing programs, an annual area-wide Communication Skills Workshop is most beneficial and much more practical than each parish program individually arranging its own workshop.

Meeting No. 4
In-Training Session and Mass
The fourth leadership preparation meeting is a table-discussion leaders "in-training" session wherein they experience a foreshortened version and explanation of each phase of a typical meeting. The Appendix G Home Reading Guide Series I, Meeting #8 indicates the theme, tape title, questions and Scripture praying passage for this in-training session. These guide sheets with study questions for discussion are important in a parish program.

After this mini-meeting experience, the discussion leader-teams are encouraged to share their reasons for selecting their particular biblical table-names.

In the event that the program participants have been pre-registered, the discussion leaders are given a list of the individuals at their respective tables, which includes names, addresses and telephone numbers. They are also given a sufficient number of blank roster forms (Appendix D) and welcoming handouts (Appendix E) for their table members. These forms are filled out by the discussion leaders, and given to each of their table members at the first parish meeting. The discussion leaders are requested to call each person pre-assigned to their table to confirm their registration in the program, to remind them of the first meeting's date and time, and to tell them the biblical name of their respective table-group. Scripture Programs that do not have pre-registration of participants will have to complete the rosters and welcoming handouts during the first meeting.

Finally, the first parish Scripture Program meeting is outlined for the leaders' information.

This last leadership preparation meeting is appropriately concluded with the Celebration of the Eucharist as a prayer for the participants and needs of the parish Scripture Program.

Finances

A fee of three dollars per person for each program series (when less than a hundred participants) is adequate to cover expenses for the series. The funds are used for duplicating materials, developing tape and book resource loan-out ministries, stipends for guest speakers, etc.

Importance of Parish Publicity

If we were to single out certain preparatory tasks as more important than others, publicity would rank near the top. Every available means of publicizing your parish program should be exercised. Parishioners can be made aware of the Scripture Program through a variety of means, such as:

(1) **a parish newsletter** sent to all parishioners one month in advance of the program opening which includes an explanation of the program and a registration form;

(2) **"flyers"** distributed with the Sunday bulletins two Sundays before the opening date of the program (or place notices on the cars at all the Masses);

(3) **bulletin notices** with a registration form distributed two Sundays before the opening date of the program and notices continuing thereafter the Sunday before each meeting date;

(4) **posters** outside all church doors two weeks before the opening program date and regularly thereafter during the program year;

(5) parish priests' **homilies** giving support to the Scripture Program which are presented at all the Masses two weeks before the opening date of the program;

(6) the most rewarding means of publicity—**word of mouth and personal invitation** by those involved in the program leadership.

We utilized all of the above techniques in publicizing our first parish Scripture Program. About three weeks after the program had begun we were approached by a parishioner who said she was delighted that a program on Scripture had started, but she hadn't heard anything about it, why hadn't we publicized it? The message was clear, no matter how much publicity is offered, some people still will not get the message, due to vacations, illness, etc. . . . Use every means available within your parish and surrounding parishes to make known that Scripture is about to be studied, shared and prayed in your parish.

Importance of Maintaining Ongoing Contact and Communication

As program leaders we have found that regular "one-to-one" contact with each of our discussion leaders and job coordinators was vital to the smooth operation of the program. When possible this contact should be by means of monthly or bi-monthly leadership meetings. Such periodic meetings should include:

(1) sharing ideas on building table-group community;

(b) continuing instruction on communication and facilitation skills;

(c) sharing how specific table-discussion problems are handled;

(d) sharing new material previewed and recommended for future use;

(e) opportunities for sharing variations for praying Scripture;

(f) interpersonal support within the program leadership;

(g) social opportunities for growth in friendship and community.

Program leaders should also maintain periodic contact with the parish pastor, reporting on the progress and response of the parish Scripture Program.

We have found that continuing contact and follow-up throughout the year have resulted in strong table discussion groups that have experienced little or no attrition in membership. In those instances when we failed to consistently maintain contact with certain discussion leaders, attrition at those table groups was always higher.

Year-End Scripture Program Meetings

The last meeting of a series or for the year should provide an opportunity for the participants to pre-register for the forthcoming year's program. An invitation is also extended to both current discussion leaders and job coordinators, as well as any participants who may be interested, to sign up to become the next year's discussion leaders and job coordinators.

The last parish Scripture Program meeting of the year is a community celebration, including the Celebration of the Eucharist followed by a potluck lunch, dinner or dessert.

Program Leader's Report to the Pastor

Program leaders should submit a written year-end parish Scripture Program report to the parish pastor, including projected plans for the succeeding year's program(s).

Importance of Evaluations

We have found that soliciting early evaluations from the participants can be most helpful in keeping the program oriented to the needs of the members, as well as alerting the program leaders to potential problem areas. During the fifth meeting of a parish program the participants are invited to write a brief evaluation of their personal response to the program format, the degree of table-community growth, facilitation at tables, etc. . . . Shortly after the fifth parish meeting, a special program leadership evaluation meeting is held to evaluate all aspects of the program format, with special attention given to the participants' written evaluations.

End of Year Evaluations

A final written evaluation (see Appendix F) is requested from both table-discussion leaders and the participants during the last meeting of a series. These evaluations assist the program leadership in developing and coordinating subsequent years Scripture Programs in accord with their parishioners expressed needs and interests.

Following the last Scripture Program meeting for the year, we have always held a program leadership evaluation meeting. At this meeting we, as program leaders, present a report to the table-discussion leaders and the job coordinators on the participants final written evaluations. This is a good time to discuss areas of suggested change and/or reorganization. Some preplanning for follow-on programs should be discussed, such as:

(1) leadership organization for the coming year which should include identification of discussion leader couples or teams, and coordinators of jobs and ministries, pre-assignments of table groups, etc. . .;

(2) planning and scheduling of the publicity for the forthcoming program;

(3) scheduling of leadership preparation meetings prior to the program start dates;

(4) discussion of the theme of the next year's series and resources to be used in its development.

STRUCTURE OF A PARISH PROGRAM MEETING

The structure of a parish Scripture Program is quite similar to the home program and utilizes the same basic meeting format of study, sharing and praying Scripture as described in Chapter 2. The most significant difference is the number of participants and the techniques used during the sharing and praying phases of the meetings.

STUDY Phase

The **STUDY phase** provides the instructional input and virtually all of the study input techniques mentioned in Chapter 2, are readily adaptable for the **STUDY phase** of a parish Scripture Program.

SHARING Phase

As we have indicated earlier the parish program participants are divided into small eight to ten member groups. Where a home program can handle up to sixteen participants in a meeting, the groups in a parish program must be smaller, not only to allow each member time to share, but mainly to keep the conversational volume at a controlled level. If too large a group tries to share, either they cannot hear one another, or they must speak so loud the overall volume in the hall from all the groups becomes excessive. We have had as many as 250 people in a parish hall at 25 tables (ten to a table) and the sharing and praying phases functioned very well. The small sharing group has proved to be the catalyst wherein interested and caring people, exchanging views and witnessing to one another, grow into loving Christian communities. We can talk "at" or "to" someone indefinitely, but we will only come to know them when we share *with* them and they *with* us, over an extended period of time. As trust grows, community forms and the group is able to share more and more openly with one another. A total appreciation of the value of group sharing can only come through experience, that is when casual acquaintances become deep friendships and the stranger becomes known as a brother or sister in Christ.

In St. Luke 10:1, our Lord sent his disciples out "two by two," so also we appoint two discussion leaders with each small sharing group. In Deuteronomy 32:30, Scripture tells us two can stand ten times stronger than one, and in Ecclesiastes 4:12 we are told of the strength of two in the Lord, "a three-ply cord is not easily broken." The (table) discussion leader couple, or team (of two), provide mutual support to one another during the

SHARING phase of the meeting. They are enablers of the discussion not instructors or teachers. The table-discussion leaders share their comments, personal reflections, feelings and questions along with the other eight members of their small table community. When one leader is absent or becomes sick, the other is able to carry on and lead the discussion at their table without interruption.

The *SHARING phase* of the meeting within the table group entails discussions on the meaning of the study input, leading to individual sharing of how the material "spoke" to each of them personally. Each participant uses a notebook to keep notes on salient points, key thoughts or questions that they feel would be worth sharing or clarifying within their groups.

At the end of the *SHARING phase*, just prior to beginning the scriptural praying, we usually call for table-group summaries. Each table group selects a representative to stand before the entire assembly and give a short one-to-two minute summary of the main ideas or key points that their table discussed during the sharing time. Often new groups must be reminded that it is not necessary to summarize everything discussed during the *SHARING phase*, only one or two key ideas. As each table group makes their presentation, the entire assembly is given some idea of what was discussed at other tables, and often additional or entirely new insights are received. No one is ever forced to get up before the whole assembly, only those who volunteer or who feel comfortable in doing so.

PRAYING SCRIPTURAL Phase

The *PRAYING phase* utilizes the same basic scriptural praying methods described in Chapter 2. The selected Scripture passage is first introduced by one of the program leaders to the entire assembly, followed by the first reading of the passage. After a short meditative silence each table group begins personal sharing on how the Lord is speaking to them through the scriptural passages. One of the program leaders reads the passage a second time, and after a short meditation, each group again separately shares their reflections. Finally after the third reading and silent meditation, each group prays the passage. After the parish program has become comfortable with the basic Scripture praying method, we suggest introducing some of the variations to scriptural prayer described in Chapter 2.

Job and Ministry Coordinators

An old proverb states that, "friends divide the work and multiply the joy." Speaking from experience, two program leaders, no matter how dedicated, cannot run a parish Scripture Program as effectively alone as they can with a loving and supporting "core" community. Appendix C to this chapter outlines suggested jobs and ministries that can relieve the program leaders of a large amount of the administrative and logistic effort, and enable them to concentrate on leading the meetings. The importance of this type of assistance cannot be overemphasized. It can make the difference between either two frenzied program leaders on opening night, or such a calm and well-organized meeting that it appears to lack organization; where things just happen all at the right time and place!

Refreshments

Usually we have limited our refreshments to coffee and tea, and rarely offered cookies, cakes, etc. When the *STUDY phase* of a meeting is a taped talk we usually suggest that the participants feel free to get up anytime during the study or sharing portions of the meeting and partake of refreshments as they desire. An exception would be when a speaker provides the *STUDY phase* of the meeting, in that case the members are requested to obtain refreshments before the meeting begins or during the *SHARING phase*. We have generally discouraged refreshments during the *PRAYING SCRIPTURE phase*. Allowing the participants to move around a little during the *STUDY phase* makes even the longest tape much more bearable.

Frequency of Meetings and Length of a Series

A typical parish Scripture Program will consist of two or three series during a September through May program year. Each series can have a different theme or can be the ongoing development of a theme begun in an earlier series.

A parish daytime or nighttime program that meets weekly has a great potential for developing a theme over a single series of 18 meetings or two series adding up to 36 meetings for the year. The first series containing up to 18 meetings would begin in September and run through January, and the second series would cover February through May.

Another approach to parish weekly meetings would be having three shorter series of eight to ten meetings each. Series I would begin in September and go through early December; series II would begin in early January and go through mid-March; and series III would begin in mid-March and run through May. Shorter length series sometimes fit into parishioners' busy schedules more easily than the anticipation of a year-long commitment.

Parishes that choose to meet twice a month, usually nighttime programs, also average eight to ten meetings for each series during a September through May program year. Series I, would begin in September and run through January and series II would extend from February through May.

We have experienced, or are aware of parish programs that have fit into all the above variations. Each approach was planned with the needs of a particular group of people in mind ... and the results have been very fruitful.

Typical Meeting Timetables

As we have stressed earlier, the program leaders are organizers and coordinators of each meeting. They insure that the meetings flow smoothly and that sufficient time is allocated for each phase. Flexibility in a meeting timetable is up to the discretion of the program leaders. However, one phase of a meeting, such as the **SHARING phase**, should not be allowed to excessively overrun at the expense of the praying phase. Sufficient time should always be allowed for the adequate performance of each of the three phases of a meeting.

Meetings should start promptly and end promptly. Nothing is more discouraging than hurrying to arrive on time for a meeting only to have it start fifteen minutes late. Conversely, people often get anxious when the end is unduly drawn out due to poor planning or last minute announcements. A ***crisp timetable*** is an important asset to any meeting.

Listed below are two samples of timetables that have proven successful for a two and a half hour length meeting.

I—PARISH SCRIPTURE PROGRAM MEETING
STUDY INPUT BY TAPED TALK

TIME	ACTIVITY
5-10 minutes before meeting begins	(A) Music ministry begins group singing to settle participants into their seats *before* meeting begins.
2 minutes	(B) Meeting Begins—Opening Prayer and Introduction of the theme of the taped talk.
40 to 60 minutes	(C) **STUDY Phase of meeting:** Length of the tape determines the length of the study input, usually 40 to 60 minutes. We advise playing only half a tape for a meeting if the tape is over an hour long. (This timetable is based on a 58 min. tape.)
35 minutes	(D) **SHARING Phase of meeting:** 1. Table-group sharing utilizing suggested discussion/sharing questions as desired.
10 minutes	2. Four to five table-group summaries before the entire assembly, each less than two minutes long.

3 to 5 minutes	(E) **PRAYING SCRIPTURE Phase of meeting:**
	 1. Introductory Comments on the selected passage:
	   (a) method of praying Scripture to be used:
	   (b) THEN-context background of the passage;
	   (c) suggested aids for personal application—e.g., personal questions, symbolism, analogies ...
	   (d) first reading of passage to assembly, etc.

25 to 30 minutes	2. Praying Scripture in table-groups.
5 minutes	(F) Announcements (kept to minimum). (G) Music ministry closes meeting with appropriate song.

II—PARISH SCRIPTURE PROGRAM MEETING
STUDY INPUT: GUEST OR REGULAR SPEAKER

TIME	ACTIVITY
5 to 10 minutes before meeting begins	(A) Music ministry begins group singing to settle participants into their seats *before* starting time of meeting.
2 to 3 minutes	(B) Meeting begins—Opening Prayer and introduction of the speaker.
40 to 60 minutes	(C) **STUDY Phase of meeting:** 1. Presentation/Teaching followed by a, 2. Question and Answer Period.
35 minutes	(D) **SHARING Phase of meeting:** 1. Table-group sharing utilizing suggested discussion/sharing questions as desired.
10 to 15 minutes	2. Additional Question and Answer Period, if desired and time schedule permitting.

3 to 5 minutes	(E) **PRAYING SCRIPTURE Phase of meeting:**
	1. Introductory Comments on the selected passage:
	  (a) state method of praying Scripture to be used;
	  (b) THEN-context background of the passage;
	  (c) suggested aids for personal application—e.g., personal questions, symbolisms, analogies, etc.,
	  (d) first reading of passage to assembly, etc.

25 to 30 minutes	2. Praying Scripture in table-groups.
5 minutes	(F) Announcements (kept to minimum). (G) Music ministry closes meeting with an appropriate song (fitting theme of meeting).

ROLE OF LEADERS

During one of our leadership training meetings the participants were asked to list the qualities and attitudes they felt were essential characteristics of Christian leaders. Their responses and expectations provided excellent criteria for Scripture Program leadership consciousness. Therefore, before detailing the responsibilities of parish program leaders we want to look at the basic qualities and attitudes expected of those in responsible leadership positions.

It was unanimously agreed that a leader's most valuable and effective quality is "Love," and this is experienced by others as a Charism. In fact, when love is truly the essential attitude of Christian leaders then their leadership is Charism, that is, a gift of God given to build up the people of God into a loving community of believers.

This Charism of love in Scripture Program leaders is expressed and defined in three interrelated ways within a parish program—through *service*, with *affirmation* and by *invitation*.

Service
Leaders lovingly serve by organizing the structure of a program in such a manner that the concerns and interests of the individuals in the program are recognized as being the highest priority. Everything that is done is solely to enable the persons involved to be free to grow in their relationship with one another and Christ through their participation in the study, sharing and praying of Scripture. Christian service is always primarily person-centered rather than just task-directed.

Leadership is a "charism of love" when the leaders' service is so unobtrusive and gentle that it becomes a natural response to every aspect of the program operation and the needs of the participants. One's manner of serving in leadership, whether as a program leader, discussion leader or a job coordinator, should always enable the participants to focus on the purpose of their coming together and never become a distraction from that purpose.

The various roles of leadership within the program structure are of equal importance and value when the leaders' love of God and neighbor is the motivating influence for that service. Love makes the difference. Love makes every manner of service, be it leading the program or setting up the tables and chairs, a genuine Charism for building up a spirit of Christian community.

Affirmation
Affirmation by the leaders is the loving catalyst that reveals to another person his or her potential gifts of leadership. An affirming person "sees" with eyes of faith, hope and love into the abilities, talents and desires that are hidden and waiting to be called forth in the other individual. It is truly a Charism of love to help another person believe they can do for others what you, as a leader, have done for them!

One of the leaders most affirming actions is to bring to the whole assembly's attention the presence of God among them as they share with one another at their table groupings. They experience affirmation as they are encouraged to look, see and hear what is happening within their sharing groups. Affirmation is an essential ingredient for personal growth spiritually and psychologically. A special gift of love that leaders can give program members is the personal affirmation that enables them to experience the reality of God's personal love and acceptance of them as they are at this moment. When leaders encourage, compliment and affirm program members, personal renewal, inner healing, psychological maturation and spiritual freedom are always experienced!

Invitation
The heart of leadership is the ability to help others recognize their own gifts and talents. This discovery is often begun by the leader's approach which simply and openly invites them to come together—to share their lives and to pray together. Most potential program leaders, discussion leaders and coordinators of any job in a program, begin to believe they can do what they are capable of doing, *after* someone believes enough in them to invite them to use their gifts for the benefit of others. The continued development of ongoing home or parish programs will always find its leadership within the membership. At the end of each program year a general invitation is extended to all participants to sign up in the area of leadership in which they are interested. This general invitation is always followed by a personal one-on-one contact and affirmation by the program leaders.

Responsibilities of Leaders
The roles of the program leader couple or team of a parish program have similar responsibilities to the home program leaders. They have the overall responsibility for the organization and administration of the program, as well as the efficient functioning of each meeting. We have found through experience that a large parish size program cannot be run effectively by a committee, but can be most successful when managed by a team of two. They have the final responsibility for the satisfactory performance of all of the supporting jobs and ministries, including arrangements for audio-visual equipment. The program leaders are responsible for establishing the study input themes, preparing the home reading guides, selecting the passages for scriptural praying and previewing all new material.

While the table-discussion leaders have the responsibility for maintaining contact with their table members, the program leaders are responsible for insuring continual liaison with each of their table-discussion leaders. In the event of a table discussion leader's continued absence, prompt follow-up by the program leaders has proven to be a reliable means of resolving potential problems before they get out of hand.

The table-discussion leaders are generally responsible for their small table community. They have the responsibility for insuring the table sharings function smoothly and stay on the subject of the meeting. They maintain contact with the members of their table, calling beforehand to remind them of the forthcoming meetings, and contacting any absent members to give them the next meeting's home reading guide as well as any other announcements. This one-to-one contact gives the participants a sense of community support. Nothing is sadder than to have a member return after a prolonged absence or illness and relate that during their time of need no one from their Christian group bothered to inquire about or visit them. We must be sensitive to one another, most especially in times of need.

Community Building
As with the home programs, one of the greatest aids to building community spirit outside of the regular program meetings are periodic potluck dinners, special evenings set aside for fellowship, or holiday and special occasion

parties. These special affairs can be limited to just the table discussion leaders and job coordinators or occasionally expanded to include the entire program membership as circumstances permit. A once or twice a year Celebration of the Eucharist can also enhance the spirit of community that is growing within the program.

A couple of years ago we felt the need for special activities for community building in an area-size program we were leading, since the 150 members came from 41 different parishes! Many drove long distances to the program so they were able to see each other only at the weekly morning meetings. At the beginning of the program year, in September, we invited all members to set aside the first Tuesday of each month and to bring sack lunches and stay after the meeting and visit with each other within their table groups or with other community members. On the third Tuesday of each month (during the program year) we also scheduled a program leadership meeting immediately after the morning meeting. Discussion leaders and job coordinators were also encouraged to bring their sack lunches that day and plan to stay after the meeting to visit. Many new friendships were begun and deepened over sack lunches that year and the entire program membership experienced the growth of the spirit of real Christian community; leading one member to describe their program experience in the words of St. Paul in Ephesians 4:15–16, "Let us profess the truth in love and grow to the full maturity of Christ the Head. Through him the whole body grows, and with the proper functioning of the members joined firmly together by each supporting ligament, builds itself up in love" (NAB). That truly expresses the exercise and experience of the Charism of love that should be the aim of all persons involved in Scripture Program leadership.

FIRST-YEAR THEME DEVELOPMENT AND TYPICAL MEETINGS

As in the home group's initial year, the parish Scripture Program's first year study input will usually be a series of taped talks on the *"Overview of the Old and New Testaments."* We have incorporated home reading guides into our parish level programs as an aid to enhance member participation. The Home Reading Guides were initiated at the request of our first parish program membership. Since then program leaders of other home and parish Scripture Programs have expressed their appreciation for the reading guides, finding them a major asset in their programs. The guides' assigned home readings and scriptural prayer passages prepare the participants for greater receptivity during the study phase of the meetings. Discussion and sharing questions enable the discussion leaders to facilitate the sharing with greater confidence. Home Reading Guides are included at the end of this chapter (Appendix G) for the purpose of assisting groups choosing to use Father Richard Rohr's taped talks on the overview of the Old and New Testaments.

Refer to the home Scripture Program chapter's "first year theme development" for the resources and meeting outlines that are also applicable for a first-year parish program that utilizes taped talks as its primary study input.

Introductory First Meeting of a Parish Program

The first meeting of a program series is appropriately an opportunity for members to become acquainted and program leaders to explain the purpose and format of the Scripture Program.

The program registrants are directed to their assigned tables, each of which displays a biblical name-card. The discussion leaders provide each of their table members with a roster of table members (Appendix D), a handout explaining the program (Appendix E) and a handout containing the first and second meetings' Home Reading Guides (Appendix G).

After opening the meeting with prayer, the program leaders introduce themselves and the table-discussion leaders. Five minutes is then taken for the discussion leader-teams to share with their table members why they chose their table's biblical name.

At this point the individual table groups get acquainted for about 15 minutes by means of a group-dynamic "diad." Using a one-to-one approach, each member acquaints him/herself with the person next to him/her. After five minutes of the one-to-one sharing, the discussion leaders call all the members of their table group together and each of the ten members introduce their new friend to the rest of the group, going around the table until everyone has been introduced. This usually takes another ten minutes.

The program leaders then call the entire membership together to give a 30 minute explanation of the goals and format of the program. Each phase of study, sharing and praying is explained. A summary of this explanation is in the handout given to the members at the beginning of the meeting. The program leaders may want to add further information on the development of their particular program up to this point in time. The next 30 to 60 minutes (as time permits) is allocated for the table groups to deepen their new found friendships especially by sharing the suggested questions contained in the reading guide for the first meeting (Appendix G).

The program leaders begin the final 30 minutes of the meeting with a brief explanation of the method to be used for praying Scripture, and the introduction of the chosen passage, followed by Scripture prayer. Announcements and a closing prayer bring the first parish Scripture meeting to an end.

Included in the suggested Home Reading Guides (Appendix G) for the outline of meeting No. 1 is a choice of two sets of discussion/sharing questions and a passage for Scripture prayer. Either set is suitable for a first year (or an ongoing) program's initial meeting. We've used No. 1 (a) set for the first meeting of our first-year program, and the alternate (b) set at the beginning of the second- or third-year programs.

A Typical Meeting

A typical parish Scripture Program meeting opens with song led by the music-ministry, followed by the program leader's prayer for God's blessing upon the participants and their time to be spent together. The study input presentation, the introduction of the Scripture passage and the three scriptural readings during the praying phase are presented from a podium before the entire assembly. The sharing and praying phases are done within the table groups.

The speaker and his/her topic, the taped talk, or the audio-visual media is introduced by the program leaders and the **STUDY phase** begins. Normally, this phase of the meeting averages an hour to an hour and a quarter, followed by a 45 minute **SHARING phase** and a 30 minute praying phase, for a total of two and a half hours.

The flexibility within a parish meeting is somewhat limited in that adequate time must be allowed for each phase while still beginning and ending on time. The program leaders maintain the smooth flow of the meeting through the three phases by being sensitive and discerning when to move on into the next phase. When a speaker is "entertaining" questions, it may be necessary to remind him/her that "The next question should be the last" as the time for the **STUDY phase** draws to an end. It is important that the **STUDY phase** does not infringe upon the **SHARING phase**, or the **SHARING phase** limit the time for **PRAYING SCRIPTURE**. Each phase is important to the meeting and sufficient time should be allocated for each when scheduling the meeting.

As the sharing time draws to an end the transition into the next phase is smoothed by the program leader reminding the participants that they "have two minutes left to draw their sharings to a conclusion." At this point the program leaders call for brief table summaries which provide the entire assembly with some of the key thoughts shared at the various tables. In a parish size program it is almost inevitable that each time a program leader steps up to the microphone, it will be an interruption to someone's sharing. During the praying phase the interruption of the sharings is softened by simply announcing the "second reading" or "third reading," pausing for half a minute for the room to become silent, before proceeding to the next reading. The program leader signals the end of the praying phase by stepping to the microphone, saying "Amen" and pausing a minute for the individual groups to conclude their prayers.

Announcements are made, and Home Reading Guides are distributed during the final five to ten minutes of the meeting before the music ministry leads the participants in closing prayer and song. Fellowship follows the meeting as long as it is convenient for members to remain.

ALTERNATE STUDY INPUT APPROACHES AND DEVELOPMENT OF THEMES

Many first-year parish Scripture Programs must rely primarily upon sets of taped talks for their study input. For follow-on programs that choose to continue using taped talks the abundance of resources and choice of themes offers sufficient study input for many future years of programming. For ideas, see the "suggested themes and related resources" section of the Home Scripture Program chapter. There is no shortage of resources!

However, when there are speakers available, their participation is usually preferable. Following are four alternate approaches to the use of taped talks as the sole study input. In each of these alternate approaches, the majority of the teachings in a series are given by regular or guest speakers, or program members. Additional resources are listed in some of the approaches to suggest other possibilities available for choosing themes and sources of study input.

ALTERNATIVE NO. 1

A well-received approach to the **STUDY input** for a parish or area-wide Scripture Program is to **coordinate a balanced selection of taped talks and speakers** in developing the chosen theme. The theme and set of taped talks must be adaptable enough to allow for the interjecting of teachings between the individual taped talks. The set of taped talks provides the basic theme, with the speakers adding further insight and depth of information to the subject matter. It takes time to coordinate both speakers and tapes while maintaining continuity with the series' theme. However, the enrichment received is well worth the extra effort required of the program leaders.

Some suggested Scripture sets of taped talks that provide this kind of general theme and flexibility are:

Great Themes of Scripture: Overview of the Old Testament by Rev. Richard Rohr, O.F.M.,

Jesus and His Church: Overview of the New Testament by Rev. Richard Rohr, O.F.M.,

Toward Understanding the New Testament Series by eight Scripture scholars,

The Prophets: Charismatic Men by Rev. Carroll Stuhlmueller, C.P.,

Gospel of Mark by Rev. Donald Senior,

Gospel of Matthew by Joseph Grassi,

Gospel of Luke by Joseph Grassi,

Gospel of John by Stephen Doyle,

Paul: The Proclaimer by Rev. Eugene LaVerdiere, S.S.S.

Following are two examples of Scripture Programs that used this approach. Both of these programs used the "Great Themes of Scripture" and "Jesus and His Church" sets of taped talks by Father Richard Rohr, O.F.M., to establish their general theme of an overview of the Old and New Testament.

Example No. 1—A Regular Speaker and Taped Talks, Equal Ratio

This example is taken from a first-year parish program that met in the evening. In addition to the taped talks, a parish priest added further indepth teachings on the topic of each tape. The taped talks were used approximately every other meeting, with the priest giving his teachings subsequent to the taped presentation. His teaching added deeper insight and further development of some aspect of the topic of the taped talk. A question and answer period was utilized after his teachings. The response of the program's 160 participants confirmed to us the value of this approach. The use of taped talks for half of the study input reduced the pressure on the priest and the amount of preparation required for this weekly program series.

Example No. 2—Guest Speakers and Taped Talks, Two-to-One Ratio

This example is patterned after a first-year multi-parish program that met in the daytime. As an area program, there was a greater opportunity to reach into the diocese, inviting laity, religious and clergy to present teachings to augment the taped talks for two series during a program year. Twenty-three guest speakers responded with Scripture teachings that brought tremendous insight and added depth to the overall theme of the program. The 120 ladies participating in the program unanimously concurred at the end of the program year that this approach had given them a solid Catholic Scripture foundation in their lives as adult Christians. Their evaluation of the speakers and taped talks was outstanding and highly supportive.

In the following series' outlines the teachings given by the guest speakers are marked with an asterisk (*). These listings of the speaker's topics interspersed with the tapes show how a number of speakers can be brought into this type of approach, selecting similar or complementary topics to develop a series' theme. It is exciting to see and imagine what can be done by innovative program leaders!

OVERVIEW OF THE GREAT THEMES OF THE OLD TESTAMENT

Meeting #1   *Explanation of the Scripture Program Purpose and Format*
    by Program Leaders

Meeting #2   Tape, *The Call: Introduction to the Word*
    by Rev. Richard Rohr, O.F.M.

Meeting #3   Tape, *Brotherhood, A New Way of Living: Praying Scripture*
    by Msgr. David Rosage, S.J.

Meeting #4   Tape, *Exodus—The Journey of Faith*
    by Rev. Richard Rohr, O.F.M.

Meeting #5   *Teaching, *Covenant Living: Law, Love and the Promised Land*
    by Guest Speaker

Meeting #6   Tape, *Joshua to Kings: Ordinary Becomes Extraordinary*
    by Rev. Richard Rohr, O.F.M.

Meeting #7   *Teaching, *Listening Men of God: Judges and Kings*
    by Guest Speaker

Meeting #8   Tape, *The Prophets: Radical Traditionists*
    by Rev. Richard Rohr, O.F.M.

Meeting #9   *Teaching, *Prophet Hosea: Call to be a Prophet of Love*
    by Guest Speaker

Meeting #10   *Teaching, *Prophets Jeremiah, Ezekiel and Isaiah: Prophets of Promise*
    by Guest Speaker

Meeting #11   Tape, *Genesis: God and Man*
    by Rev. Richard Rohr, O.F.M.

Meeting #12   *Teaching, *God's Creative Love: Genesis 1–11*
    by Guest Speaker

Meeting #13   *Teaching, *Living A Faith-Filled Life: Genesis 12–50*
    by Guest Speaker

Meeting #14   *Teaching, *Wisdom Literature: The Book of Wisdom*
    by Guest Speaker

Meeting #15   *Teaching, *The Psalms for Today*
    by Guest Speaker

Meeting #16   Tape, *Job: Good and Evil*
    by Rev. Richard Rohr, O.F.M.

Meeting #17   *Teaching, *The Women of the Old Testament*
    by Guest Speaker

Meeting #18   Tape, *Salvation History: Faith in Evolution*
    by Rev. Richard Rohr, O.F.M.

OVERVIEW OF THE GREAT THEMES OF THE NEW TESTAMENT

Meeting #1   Tape, *Matthew's Good News: The Reign of God*
    by Rev. Richard Rohr, O.F.M.

Meeting #2   *Teaching, *Jesus: The Way to the Father*
    by Guest Speaker

Meeting #3   *Teaching, *Jesus: Eucharist and Life*
    by Guest Speaker

Meeting #4   *Teaching, *Healing Ministry of Christ in the Church*
    by Guest Speaker

Meeting #5   *Teaching, *The Divine Humor of God*
    by Guest Speaker

Meeting #6   Tape, *Mark and John: Jesus Is Lord*
    by Rev. Richard Rohr, O.F.M.

Meeting #7   *Teaching, *Christ's Teaching on Christian Living and Morality*
    by Guest Speaker

Meeting #8   *Teaching, *The Beatitudes and Christian Life*
    by Guest Speaker

Meeting #9   Tape, *Luke and Acts: A New Gift*
    by Rev. Richard Rohr, O.F.M.

Meeting #10   *Teaching, *Jesus: Last Discourse: Call to Discipleship and Love*
    by Guest Speaker

Meeting #11   *Teaching, *Jesus: Man of Prayer*
    by Guest Speaker

Meeting #12   *Teaching, *Resurrection and Pentecost: Christ Alive and With Us!*
    by Guest Speaker

Meeting #13   Tape, *Paul: A New Life in Christ*
    by Rev. Richard Rohr, O.F.M.

Meeting #14   *Teaching, *Themes from First Corinthians*
    by Guest Speaker

Meeting #15   *Teaching, *Themes from Ephesians*
    by Guest Speaker

Meeting #16   Tape, *Apocalypse: The New Creation*
    by Rev. Richard Rohr, O.F.M.

Meeting #17   *Teaching, *Mary—Revealed in Scripture*
    by Guest Speaker

Meeting #18   *Holy Land Slide Presentation and Sharing About Trip*
    by Guest Speaker
    Celebration of the Eucharist: Thanksgiving for the Year
    Concluding with Potluck Lunch

ALTERNATIVE NO. 2

A favored approach to the **STUDY phase** of a parish Scripture Program is scheduling **a regular speaker for a series of meetings**. This approach allows the speaker to choose the theme and appropriate resources for its development.

Some of the themes frequently selected by speakers include one of the Gospels, an Epistle, the Psalms, the Acts of the Apostles and the book of Revelation. To assist speakers in their choice of themes and resources, refer them to the "suggested themes and related resources" section of the Home Scripture Program chapter.

In this approach the speaker develops a series of homiletic or commentary style presentations over a pre-determined number of meetings. Home Reading Guides are prepared by the speaker based on the content of his/her presentation.

Some speakers choose resource material that determines the program theme, i.e., a specific Scripture commentary or study guide, the Sunday liturgical readings, etc. Their presentations/teachings expand upon the material available in the selected resource book. Scripture readings are also suggested for regular home reading preparation by the participants.

In addition to the meetings planned by the speaker, the program leaders can add several additional meetings to include an initial program explanation, one or more taped talks and/or audio-visual presentations and the Celebration of the Eucharist to complete the series. Allowing for the use of one or more taped talks or audio-visuals within a series of meetings provides a degree of flexibility for the speaker which can be especially helpful in case of emergency that may keep him/her from giving a presentation at a specific meeting.

Following are two examples that show how a regular speaker can develop a Scripture theme through his/her presentations and the use of complementary resources.

Example No. 1

In this example the Scripture Program schedule allowed for a series of thirteen weekly meetings. A speaker was available to present nine teachings on the Gospel of Luke. To fill out the series and complement the nine basic teachings, two additional guest speakers were invited to present teachings on specific themes in Luke's Gospel, and a single taped talk and a filmstrip were also added. If any of the speakers would have had to cancel their teaching, the tape or A-V would have been the substituted study input for that meeting. Since there were no unexpected cancellations, both study inputs were used at the final two meetings of the series.

THEME: THE GOSPEL OF LUKE

Series' length: 13 meetings.
Resources: regular speaker, two guest speakers, books, a taped talk and an audio-visual.

BOOKS:
Invitation to Luke: A Commentary, R. Karris
Read and Pray Series: The Gospel of St. Luke, R. Karris
Nesting in the Rock, G. Maloney, S.J. (for meeting #6)

TAPED TALK:
The Poor Church in Luke's Gospel, R. Karris

AUDIO-VISUAL:
Luke—Prayer and Social Apostolate, P. Perkins

Meeting Study Input Outline:

Meeting #1 *Explanation of Scripture Program Format and Get Acquainted Time*
by Program Leader

Meeting #2 Teaching, *Personal Growth through the Scriptures for Christian Evangelization*
by Guest Speaker

Meeting #3 Teaching, "Roots"
by Regular Speaker

Meeting #4 Teaching, "Some Seed Fell Among . . ."
by Regular Speaker

Meeting #5 Teaching, "Luke, Our Beloved Physician Sends You Greetings . . ."
by Regular Speaker

Meeting #6 Teaching, "Abandonment to Our Heavenly Father's Love"
by Guest Speaker

Meeting #7 Teaching, "Sent to Bring Glad Tidings . . ."
by Regular Speaker

Meeting #8 Teaching, *Commission: Reflections on a Biblical Genre*
by Regular Speaker

Meeting #9 Teaching, *Signs of the Kingdom and Summons to Discipleship*
by Regular Speaker

Meeting #10 Teaching, *The Western Gate and the Highest of the Hills*
by Regular Speaker

Meeting #11 Teaching, "A Savior Has Been Born . . . ." *The Messiah and Lord*
by Regular Speaker

Meeting #12 Tape, *The Poor Church in Luke's Gospel*
by Rev. Robert Karris

Meeting #13 Filmstrip, *Luke—Prayer and Social Apostolate*
by Pheme Perkins
Celebration of Eucharist in Thanksgiving for Series
Potluck Lunch to conclude Series I.

Example No. 2

A most enriching theme that can be developed for an ongoing Scripture Program is *"The Sunday Liturgical Readings."* A speaker provides the weekly teachings based on the theme of the liturgical readings for the forthcoming Sunday's liturgy. Either a regular speaker or a team of two to four speakers, taking turns, provides the weekly teachings. The parish Sunday missalettes provide the weekly liturgical home readings for the program members for their private study and scriptural praying.

The speaker prepares the **SHARING phase** discussion questions based on his/her teaching and the home readings. One of the three readings or the responsorial Psalm is selected for the praying phase of the meeting.

Numerous Scripture commentaries and study guides are available to provide the necessary background information on the liturgical readings and to assist in the preparation of the teachings. Of special note are:

Biblical Notes for the Sunday Lectionary, by Rev. James Gaffney, and two liturgical subscription resources:

Scripture in Church (a subscription quarterly magazine),

Discover the Bible (a subscription weekly leaflet).

Refer to the last chapter resources under "book" listings and "Sunday Liturgical Reading Guides" for further information.

Using this approach, over a three-year cycle the biblical themes that weave throughout Scripture are disclosed and much of the Old and New Testament is studied, shared and prayed. Individuals have shared that this approach to Scripture study and prayer has enabled them to discover new meaning, depth and "Life" in the Sunday Liturgy!

A priest in one parish has led a "Liturgical Bible Study" for several years. He prepares a bi-weekly "Bible Newsletter" that covers the content of his teachings on the background of the liturgical readings and includes reflections for personal application of the Word. His teaching is given on Mondays so the participants in the program have the balance of the week for personal study and prayer on the liturgical passages before hearing them "anew" from the pulpit on Sunday. He has given permission for his name and address to be included herein; and anyone wishing to contact him for further information on his approach to "Liturgical Bible Study," may do so by writing to Rev. Thomas Welbers, Our Lady of Lourdes, 9800 Canby Ave., Northridge, California 91324, (213) 349-1500.

ALTERNATIVE NO. 3

A very practical and enjoyable way of providing the program study input is to have *regular teachings given by members of the program.* Two to four members join together as a team of speakers. This approach requires greater pre-program preparation and cooperation. The (speaker) team members choose a theme and select a compatible Scripture commentary or study guide that will be recommended to the program participants for their home reading. Each speaker selects the teachings he/she will prepare and present. The teachings can be based primarily upon the content of the selected Scripture commentary/study guide, or developed beyond the scope of that content using other resources. Each speaker also selects a compatible Scripture passage and prepares an introduction of that passage for the praying phase of the meeting. When necessary, Home Reading Guides and discussion/sharing questions are also prepared by the speakers, based on the content of his/her teaching. Usually the team members give teachings in rotation, each assuming responsibility for two or more meetings within a series. As a team, they substitute for one another in emergencies, as well as provide support for each other in the preparation and presentation of their individual teachings.

Not only is it a joy to hear and see your own program members giving the teachings, but often a fellow-participant becomes the catalyst of God's Word, helping it to find "Life" within our hearts because we can personally relate to the speaker as one of us! For the speakers, team-teaching is a fantastic catalyst for teacher-training, providing the motivation and support to develop one's abilities and gifts for teaching God's Word for others!

Following are Scripture commentaries and study guides that are well suited for this approach. Each has discussion questions and the three annotated with an asterisk have Scripture references for home reading and prayer.

*Discovering the Bible: Eight Keys for Learning and Praying, by Rev. John Tickle

Reading the New Testament: An Introduction, by Pheme Perkins

*Who Do You Say That I Am?, by Rev. Edward Ciuba

*A Commentary on the Gospel of Matthew, by Rev. Albert Kirk and Rev. Robert Obach

Invitation to Matthew, by Rev. Donald Senior

Invitation to Mark, by Paul Achtemeier

Invitation to Luke, by Rev. Robert Karris

Invitation to John, by George MacRae

Alive in the Spirit: The Church in the Acts of the Apostles, by Thomas Smith

An example of this team-teaching approach was used by a parish that had an established Scripture Program for several years. Leaders of the parish Scripture Program saw the need for repeating an introductory Scripture course for new participants. A basic scriptural foundation was found to be essential to enable the people to appreciate and fully participate in the more indepth Scripture studies of the ongoing program. An eight-week introductory Scripture course was prepared that could be repeated periodically as needed. Only after completing the introductory program could the new members move into the ongoing program.

Four experienced program members (laity and clergy) joined together to team-teach an overview of the Old and New Testaments, each member giving two of the eight teachings. Following is an outline of the study input for the meetings and their resources. Both books were recommended to the program members for their home reading and Scripture prayer, respectively.

THEME: DISCOVERING THE BIBLE

Series' length: 8 meetings (could also be extended to 16 meetings).
Resources: teachings by team-speakers, two books.

> BOOKS:
> *Discovering the Bible: Eight Simple Keys for Learning and Praying,* by Rev. John Tickle
> *Speak Lord, Your Servant Is Listening,* by Msgr. David Rosage, S.J.
>
> Study-Input Outline (based on chapters of *Discovering the Bible*):

Meeting #1   Chapters 1 and 2, *Revelation in the Old and New Testament,*

Meeting #2   Chapters 3 and 4, *Election in the Old and New Testament,*

Meeting #3   Chapters 5 and 6, *Covenant in the Old and New Testament,*

Meeting #4   Chapters 7 and 8, *Law in the Old and New Testament,*

Meeting #5   Chapters 9 and 10, *Sin in the Old and New Testament,*

Meeting #6   Chapters 11 and 12, *Redemption in the Old and New Testament,*

Meeting #7   Chapters 13 and 14, *Messiah in the Old and New Testament,*

Meeting #8   Chapters 15 and 16, *Love in the Old and New Testament.*

ALTERNATIVE NO. 4

Lyman Coleman's Serendipity approaches to studying and sharing Scripture are "especially useful with the teachings of Jesus in the Gospels or with the Epistles." Serendipity's eight creative techniques for Bible study and 36 structured Scripture sessions, called "Value Clarifications" (12), "Scripture Happenings" (12), and "Scripture Heavies" (12), are interchangeable for developing a theme over a period of meetings or can be used individually for enrichment during a specific meeting within a series.

We have used Serendipity Scripture approaches with both adult groups and youth (teenagers) groups with enthusiastic responses. They are adaptable for small home groups, as well as the small sharing groups within a larger parish program. We have found them especially useful for getting acquainted with one another and facilitating sharing during the early stages of a program. Following are two examples of how to adapt the Serendipity Scripture sessions within the Scripture Program's threefold format of study, sharing and praying. A third example describes a meeting using Serendipity techniques adapted for a community building experience.

Example No. 1—Single Meeting Using Serendipity Approach for SHARING Phase

To augment the topic of a single meeting within a series, select a Serendipity Scripture session that complements the Scripture theme developed during the study input of the meeting. Allow time after the study input (teaching by a speaker or taped talk) to fill out the Serendipity questionnaire and then encourage that the group sharing be based on the members' answers concerning the Scripture passage in the questionnaire. Conclude the meeting with Scripture prayer, using the same passage that was studied and shared.

For example, if the meeting theme is *"The Beatitudes,"* the study input of the meeting could be a taped talk, *"Christian Living and the Beatitudes"* by Rev. Patrick Crowley, SS.CC. A complementary Serendipity Scripture Heavy would be one entitled *"A Winning Mental Attitude: Matthew 5:3–10,"* which focuses on the personal meaning of the Beatitudes in one's life.

Example No. 2—A Series Using Serendipity Scripture Approaches

A series of up to 24 meetings, coordinating Serendipity "creative Bible study techniques," and "structured Scripture sessions" can develop a theme on *"The Teachings of Jesus and Christian Living."* A regular speaker, or a member of a team of speakers from the program membership, can give teachings of 20 to 30 minutes in length for the study input. The teachings expand on the same Scripture topic that is to be used in the Serendipity Scripture session during the **SHARING phase** of the meeting. Following the teaching, the participants are given the Serendipity questionnaires and time is allowed for them to be filled out. Small group sharing follows, based on the members' written answers. The meeting concludes with Scripture prayer, using the same Scripture passage studied and shared in the earlier phases of the meeting.

One parish used this approach for a year long (September through May) daytime Scripture program, with outstanding response from their hundred-plus ladies! Four members of the program joined together as a speakers-team, taking turns preparing and presenting the teachings.

Example No. 3—Serendipity Community-Building Experience

One parish program, early in its third year, experienced that while the members of their table communities were growing closer and more sensitive to one another, little growth had occurred between the table-groups. Many program members did not know the other members outside of their own table community. The program leaders and several of the discussion leaders developed a Serendipity community-building meeting that they hoped would enable the total membership to become better acquainted and develop a fuller awareness of their parish community within the program membership.

To insure that new members had time to become comfortable with the usual meeting format, the leaders chose to wait until the fifth meeting for the Serendipity experience. Some of the most deeply touched were persons who had come to the special meeting with reservations ("I came to study Scripture, not to play games..."). The general response was enthusiastic as strangers became friends and the spirit of community grew. A variety of Serendipity crowd breakers, communication and affirmation exercises, and a structured Scripture session were used concluding with a koinania experience from Lyman Coleman's "Encyclopedia of Serendipity."

The hall clocks were covered and members were asked to remove their watches. The leaders allowed flexibility in the timing and the selection of exercises, deleting some of the "games" when they sensed the groups were ready to move on, so that sufficient time was allowed for the climax of the meeting in the Scripture sharing and koinania phases. During the koinania phase the leaders asked the group members to take the last part of the Scripture sharing a step further and show their personal support for each other. Some members took turns praying for each member of their group, while others first shared their personal needs and goals and then interlocked arms and prayed as a group. A lot of healthy crying and loving was experienced!

Following is the meeting schedule of the Serendipity exercises and the Scripture session. They are listed by title and page reference, so the reader should refer to the encyclopedia for further information on how to use each effectively. Any adaptations are explained in the schedule. The time schedule is flexible and is given as a general guide to insure sufficient time is allotted for each phase within the two and a half hour meeting.

Serendipity Community-Building Meeting Outline:

7:25 — Music Ministry (music played as members take their places).

7:30 — Introduction: Goal of Community-Building presented by the program leaders.
CROWD BREAKING (going from groups of two to eight).
Introduction, page 28.
Warm-Up: SHOULDER RUB-DOWN, page 41.
Song: "WE ARE ONE IN THE SPIRIT," page 47.

8:00 — HISTORY GIVING—1st Base, page 25.

1+1 (A) Pick a person you do not know and tell him/her as much as you can about yourself in thirty seconds; let your partner do the same.
(B) BACK-TO-BACK, page 71.

2+2 (A) Join a second group of two that you do not know, forming a group of four.
Introduce your partner to the two new people in your group, giving everyone a chance to introduce his/her partner.
(B) BUZZ-FIZZ, page 54.
(C) FOUR FACTS–ONE LIE, page 72.

4+4 (A) Join a second group of four that your group does not know, forming a group of eight.
(B) ONE FROG, page 54.
(C) SENTENCE COMPLETION, page 58.
1. If I could visit any place in the world....
2. If I could ask God one question I would ask....
3. If I knew I had only a year to live, I would spend the year....

8:30 — AFFIRMATION—2nd Base, page 26.
In groups of eight:
(A) COLORS, page 86.
(B) SCULPTURING, page 53. With your original partner (of 1+1), give your partner a facial expression that best fits his/her personality. Back in the group of eight, do a large group

	sculpture that describes one word, i.e., celebration, joy, community or love.
	(C) *SCRIPTURE NAME*, page 74. On a piece of paper assign a biblical person's name to each member of your group; and share within the group why you have chosen the biblical name for that person.
9:00	*GOAL SETTING*—3rd Base, page 27.
	(A) *PICTURE ASSOCIATION*, page 63.
	(B) *SCRIPTURE HAPPENING #4: "GOING FOR IT,"* page 184. Read Matthew 14:22–23, Jesus walks on the water. Have each person answer each question and then share their answers.
	(1) If I had been Peter when Jesus invited him to step out of the boat and walk on the water, I probably would have (circle one): a. shrunk back in horror, b. made some excuse, c. asked someone else to go first, d. explained I was just kidding, e. jumped at the chance.
	(2) If I could count on the support of the others in my group, I would like to (circle one): a. make a new commitment of my life to Christ, b. find out what God wants with my life, c. go deeper with Christ, d. stand up for what I believe, e. get involved in some kind of action.
	(3) The next risky step in my life with Christ is . . .
9:30	*KOINANIA*—Home plate, page 27. Before beginning this next phase, ask if there is anyone who has to leave early. If so, ask that he/she please do so now, so as not to disturb others during the final session. Within their group of eight, each member is asked to show his/her personal support for each other member in their group in whatever way they wish.
10:00	Scheduled end of the meeting. Groups should remain together until they have each completed their "koinania."

ONGOING DEVELOPMENT OF PARISH SCRIPTURE PROGRAMS

Following are two organizational approaches for parish Scripture Programs continuing beyond the initial introductory first year program.

A Single Ongoing Parish Scripture Program

If only one parish Scripture Program is to be offered from the second year on, the themes can be developed in accordance with any one of the previously suggested approaches. New participants are welcomed anytime during the year and merged into existing table-groups. New members should be offered the opportunity to borrow the first-year taped talks from the program tape loan-out library. Hopefully their home listening and personal background reading will gradually fill in what was missed by not being able to participate in the introductory first-year program.

Multiple Ongoing Parish Scripture Programs

There will always be newly interested parishioners who would benefit from the experience of an introductory overview of the Old and New Testaments in a first-year program. Sometimes new members entering into a more experienced ongoing program have expressed the difficulty they felt in trying to "catch-up" with those who have been participating longer. Often they cannot relate to the biblical names of persons, places and events of the Old Testament that are referred to during an indepth study of a single book of Scripture. This difficulty sometimes has discouraged new members from remaining active in an ongoing second- or third-year program. "It's over my head" has been the common response when a new member does decide to drop the program.

In this section we share a vision of how parish Scripture Programs should develop progressively over several years to meet not only the growing interests and needs of their more mature membership, but also the interests and needs of new participants.

When asked, ongoing program participants eagerly suggest themes of interest and specific books of the Bible that they would like to study in future programs. There is no doubt that they would also respond enthusiastically to the opportunity to choose from among several alternate themes presented simultaneously in parish mini-programs during a program year.

Repetition of Introductory Scripture Program and Development of Ongoing Programs

The Introductory "overview . . ." should be repeated yearly, or at least every other year, for newly interested parishioners. One year it could be a daytime program, the alternate year presented as a nighttime program.

Following the first-year parish Scripture Program one or more smaller mini-programs may be developed within the larger parish community according to the themes requested by the members. The members would choose to participate in one of the smaller Scripture Program groups (eight to thirty members) according to their choice of themes and study input material. To some extent these smaller groups are similar to the home Scripture Program groups described in chapter three, which are more self-motivated and self-directed. The basic format of studying, sharing and praying Scripture would be continued in each of the smaller program groups. Both daytime and nighttime groups, meeting weekly or twice monthly, will function effectively in such an ongoing parish Scripture Program environment.

Periodic Parish Scripture Program Gatherings

Three or four times a year the participants of all the smaller program groups should gather in the parish hall for a total parish meeting. The opening meeting for the program year (in September) should be a general presentation given by the parish program leaders/coordinators and parish priests, as a way of welcoming the new and the returning participants; and to explain the program format and themes of each of the smaller groups. The end of the program year (in May) is another opportune time when all the participants should gather together to share their thanksgiving for the gifts received and to express their thanks through the Celebration of the Eucharist, followed by a potluck lunch, dinner or dessert. Other occasions for general meetings could be when special guest speakers are invited to the Introductory Scripture Program meetings. In addition to general program meetings, occasional social gatherings, i.e., holiday parties, parish picnics and Sunday afternoon potluck dinners contribute to building the community spirit among all the program participants and their families.

Through these periodic general meetings and social gatherings the parishioners' awareness of belonging to the larger parish community is maintained and strengthened, as well as witnessing to each other by their presence how "alive" God's Word is in their daily lives!

Multiple Parish Scripture Program Leadership

The parish Scripture Program leaders for the introductory first-year program should also be the coordinators for the other ongoing programs. Experienced discussion-leader teams or couples should be the program leaders for each of the smaller Scripture Program groups. In turn, there should be as many table discussion-leaders within each smaller program group as are needed to maintain a ratio of two discussion leaders for every eight participants. Job-coordinators should be enlisted according to the need and size of each of the smaller programs.

Regular (monthly) meetings are always beneficial involving the parish Scripture Program coordinators, parish priests, the smaller group program leaders and the discussion leaders from all the groups. Such planned meetings provide a regular opportunity for sharing the progress, needs and interests of each group. These meetings also offer an opportunity to discuss new material and study input approaches, as well as to cultivate community growth within the parish leadership.

Thus a parish could have one aspect of its adult education program fully committed to introducing and deepening its parishioners' involvement in Scripture study. The entire parish community should gradually be affected by those parishioners who belong to the various Scripture Programs. Their ongoing experience of studying, sharing and praying Scripture together in small groups will be exemplified by the renewal of their lives, their service and care for one another in the parish, and their deepened expectant faith for the spiritual maturation of the entire parish body. This is truly "grassroots" evangelization through simply living the "Good News"!

Example of a Multiple Parish Scripture Program Organization

As an example let us envision a parish Scripture Program that has been established for more than three years. The program's one hundred seventy-nine members have displayed a variety of interests and needs in their desire for Scripture studies. The parish sustains in the course of a program year the following mini-programs as well as an Introductory program. The mini-programs described below are based on actual programs existing in several ongoing second- and third-year parish Scripture Programs.

1. Repeated Introductory First-Year Scripture Program

With sixty participants this program has the largest attendance of all the programs. It meets weekly at night in the parish hall. New Scripture Program members are required to participate in this program before moving on into the mini-program of their choice. The theme is the *Overview of the Old and New Testaments*. Study input is shared by a team of parishioners who have been involved in the Scripture Program for several years. Occasionally, the speakers are augmented by taped talks and audio-visual aids. Their approach is the third alternate study input described earlier in this chapter.

2. The Original Home Scripture Program Group #1

The twelve members of the first home program group within the parish continue to meet two nights a month in a member's home while also sharing in the parish Scripture Program leadership. They continue to use taped talks as their primary study input as described in a typical home program meeting in chapter three. They are able to enrich their own maturation in Scripture while previewing and evaluating new sets of taped talks for possible use in the future in parish programs. At present they are using taped talks, filmstrips and a study guide to develop the theme of *The Four Gospels, A Portrait of Jesus Christ*, as described in the third alternate study input in chapter three.

3. Ongoing Scripture Mini-Program #2

This group of thirty members meets one night a week in the parish lounge. The parish priest is the regular speaker, presenting weekly teachings on the forthcoming *Sunday liturgical readings*. His approach is example no. 2 of the second alternate study input described earlier in this chapter.

4. Ongoing Scripture Mini-Program #3

This small group of ten members meet at night twice a month in a member's home. They were interested in a more personal and indepth study of the *Prophets*. This year they are preparing and sharing individual reports and teachings on each prophet. They augment their study input with individual taped talks from a series, *The Prophets, Charismatic Men*. This approach is also providing the members the opportunity for training themselves to present Scripture study teachings in the future, if the need arises in other parish programs. This approach is similar to the second alternate study input described in chapter three.

5. Ongoing Scripture Mini-Program #4

This is a weekly daytime program that provides babysitting arrangements so that young mothers may participate. The fifty-five women meet during the morning in the parish hall. The theme of *Paul, His Life and Letters* is developed by a coordinated balance of taped talks which provide the "backbone" theme, and presentations by the parish priests, several program members and an occasional guest speaker. This approach is similar to the first alternate study input described earlier in this chapter.

6. Specialized Youth Ministry Scripture Mini-Program #5

This group of eleven young people meet weekly in the home of the youth ministry program leaders. They are studying, sharing and praying *The Gospel of Matthew* during their one and a half hour meetings. The team leaders adapt the study input through their teachings, use of audio-visuals and selected study techniques. Their adaptation of the program format is described in the third example of youth ministry program development in chapter 5.

APPENDIX A
FIRST YEAR

SCRIPTURE PROGRAM REGISTRATION
COMMITMENT FORM
PARTICIPATION REGISTRATION

Name _____ Parish _____

Address _____ City _____ Zip _____

Phone No. ( ) _____

Past/Current involvement in Parish or Religious activities? _____
_____

DISCUSSION-LEADERSHIP FACILITATION COMMITMENT

Previous Scripture Program experience? _____

Sources of past Facilitation experience/training?

Name of Table-group Co-Discussion Leader/Facilitator? _____
_____

_____ Phone No. ( ) _____

I am willing to make a one year commitment from _____ **to** _____
As a table-group discussion leader/facilitator in the _____ (parish or area)
Scripture Program. Meetings will be held on _____ (frequency/day of week/time).

(Signature) _____

JOBS/MINISTRIES COORDINATION COMMITMENT

Each job/ministry needs two or more coordinators. It is not necessary to be a discussion-leader in order to be a job coordinator. If you would like to help in any area, please check areas of interest. You will be contacted to confirm your decision to help in a specific job or ministry.

_____ Secretary (collect fees, keep records, distribute handouts & typing)
_____ Refreshments (arrange, set-up, clean-up for coffee & tea)
_____ Hall Set-Up (takes 6–8 persons to set-up chairs & tables)
_____ Hall Clean-Up (takes 6–8 persons to clear hall after the meeting)
_____ Tape Loan-Out Ministry (takes 2–4 persons to coordinate the library)
_____ Book Ministry (distribution, selling & ordering of books)
_____ Music Ministry (lead singing that opens & closes meetings; guitars, etc.)
_____ Publicity (posters, bulletin notices, name tags, table-names)

Please R.S.V.P. your program commitment and/or registration by mailing this form to program leaders before _____. **You will be contacted. Thank you.**

(Program Leaders) _____

(Address) _____

(Phone No.) _____

APPENDIX B
SCRIPTURE PROGRAM DISCUSSION LEADERS' RESPONSIBILITIES

GUIDELINES FOR FACILITATING DISCUSSIONS

1. Table discussion-facilitators are participants as well as Discussion Leaders.

2. Participate in such a way that you convey to others an attitude of ease, informality and good humor. (To "set the mood" for sharing and dialogue, begin by silently and interiorly making an act of love for each of the other participants of your table-group.)

3. Facilitators are **not teachers**. Share in such a way as to enable and encourage the other participants to feel free and comfortable in sharing. Some table groups will not be self-starters and may need to be drawn out. A brief personal sharing, relating a point of the talk to the discussion-leader's life, may be the catalyst to enable others to share.

4. Facilitators may encourage participants to take notes during the talks:

a) **"Key" points** that catch their interest (e.g., a "key" thought the speaker brought to mind and the reason "why" it spoke to him/her personally).

b) **Questions** that may draw out discussion (e.g., "He spoke of 'serving others,' what are some of the ways we can serve others?").

5. Facilitate discussion on the general subject matter of the talk and how it is applicable to the lives of the participants.

(a) Questions can be used to draw the discussion back to the appropriate subject matter.

(b) State something the speaker said, give your response to it, and ask others to give their response to it (e.g., Jim, what did you think about the talk tonight? Bill, how do you see application of this to our daily life? Chris, would you want to add a point to the talk?).

(c) When questions are asked by the participants, allow the table members to respond. If no one comments facilitate responses by asking how they feel or what they think about the question.

(d) Do not open by saying, "Does anyone have anything to say?" Instead, ask a specific person directly. Avoid asking the same person more than once if possible. If one person seems to be dominating the discussion move the questions around the group.

6. After the discussion has started, let it flow. If it goes beyond the area of the talk gently bring it back to the topic. If that doesn't work, don't be afraid to say: "We've strayed a bit...." Then repeat the original point of the discussion. If it has been sufficiently explored, move into another area of discussion.

7. If a person seems upset, nervous or hesitant to respond, allow him/her the opportunity to back gracefully away from answering.

8. **Listen carefully.** Make every effort to understand what the person is saying.

9. Facilitators and participants should refrain from giving advice. Share one's personal experience in a similar situation and allow others to evaluate the sharing in relationship to their own situation.

10. Welcome reasonable opposition to your point of view, even if one doesn't agree, opposition often broadens insight.

11. Don't criticize, condemn or be judgmental! Accepting another where he/she is does not necessarily mean you agree with the point of view expressed.

CONCERN FOR YOUR TABLE-COMMUNITY

ROSTER LIST

A roster listing each of the participant's name, address, telephone number and parish is an extremely valuable tool both for the leaders and the participants. Discussion leaders should mark attendance and annotate any collection of fees on their lists. During the initial meetings of a new program, reference to a roster is useful in learning names and enhancing communication between participants.

CONTACTS THAT BUILD COMMUNITY

Discussion-leaders should call each table member between meetings. Table members can also share in this responsibility, taking turns monthly calling the rest of their table's participants between meetings. This regular contact outside the meeting time contributes to building a sense of community within the group.

Discussion-leaders should encourage periodic opportunities for their table community to meet together after or between Scripture Program meetings (e.g., lunches, home visits, family picnics, day of prayer together, etc., contribute greatly toward community-growth).

TABLE MEMBER'S ABSENCE

If a table member is absent, contact him/her within several days after the meeting. Share with him/her any pertinent points. Give the suggested reading, the next meeting date and subject matter. Offer to loan the missed taped talk. This friendly concern lets the absentee know he/she was missed and is wanted as a contributing member at their table community.

At meetings where "Suggested Reading Guides" or other handouts are distributed, keep absent member's guide/handout, giving it to her/him at the next meeting or mail it to the member before the next meeting.

DISCUSSION-LEADER'S ABSENCE

In case of your absence, contact your co-discussion leader. If you cannot make contact with her/him, please contact someone on the discussion-leader's list and ask her/him to substitute for you. Call the program leaders to let them know of the change.   (name & phone number)

OPENINGS DURING PROGRAM YEAR

If a table member leaves the program inform the program leaders and the secretary. People on a waiting list can then be notified of the available places.

At a new member's first meeting introduce her/him to table members. Sit with her/him explaining and guiding the new member through each phase of the meeting. Provide the new member with the "Explanation of Scripture Program" handout (Appendix E) and any available past reading guides of the current series.

DISCUSSION LEADERS/FACILITATORS PERSONAL PREPARATION

SUGGEST READING

Do minimum suggested background reading faithfully. It will be one of your strongest aids in facilitating discussion.

ENRICHMENT AND INDEPTH STUDY MATERIALS

Be informed regarding enrichment and indepth study materials that are recommended and available through the Scripture Program Book and tape ministries, so you can use them yourself and suggest them to others.

PRAYER

Remember the members of your table group, the Scripture Program, its leaders and participants daily in your prayers. Your personal time spent in daily prayer and with Scripture will be the source of your strongest aid in community-building leadership and discussion facilitation.

APPENDIX C
SCRIPTURE PROGRAM JOBS AND MINISTRY COORDINATORS' RESPONSIBILITIES

The smooth functioning of a parish Scripture Program is most often the result of much shared responsibility among the various supporting jobs and ministries. Each job or ministry needs several coordinators, so that by sharing with others we "divide the care and multiply the joy" of our involvement in the program. Love expressed in a willingness to serve others, coupled with dependability and faithfulness in sharing responsibilities exemplifies a living spirit of Christian community to the other program participants.

John 13:12—So after he had washed their feet, he put his cloak back on . . . he said to them, "Do you understand what I just did for you? You addressed me as 'Teacher' and 'Lord,' and fittingly enough, for that is what I am. But if I washed your feet—I who am Teacher and Lord—then you must wash each other's feet. What I just did was to give you an example: as I have done, so you must do . . . . Once you know all these things, blest will you be if you put them into practice."

Following are a number of job assignments and/or ministries that we have found most conducive to efficient program operation.

Hospitality
The hospitality coordinator is responsible for greeting people at the door before the meeting, and directing them to a registration table. After the meeting has begun, late-comers are greeted and led to a table, introduced to the discussion leaders and seated. After the meeting, the table discussion-leaders insure that the newcomers are registered by the secretary.

Secretary
The secretary (coordinator) is responsible for establishing a master attendance list of all participants by table group for each series. The secretary also sees to it that participant name-tags are prepared and that table-name cards are placed on each table before the start of each meeting and collected at the end of each meeting. We have found that one person distributing table-name cards at the beginning of each meeting, and keeping them between meetings, is much more reliable than depending upon each table group to take care of their own name-card. In a large parish meeting the table-name cards are essential in helping participants locate their respective tables. The secretary also registers and collects fees from new participants, distributes handouts to the table groups, maintains a file of previous handouts for late-comers to the program, sends a copy of the welcoming handouts explaining the program to newcomers, and provides typing for the program handouts. Programs with larger membership usually require two or more secretaries.

Refreshments
The refreshment coordinators purchase supplies, set up the refreshments before the beginning of each meeting, clean up and store the supplies after each meeting. Expenses are usually covered by donations from members partaking of the refreshments.

Meeting Area Set Up and Clean Up
These coordinators arrive early and set up tables and chairs for the meeting as well as extra tables for registrations, book and tape ministries, etc. . . . At the end of the meeting, they make certain the tables and chairs are properly stored and the meeting area is left in order. They usually solicit additional help as needed from those present before and after the meeting.

Music Ministry
One or more members provide music for the opening and closing of each meeting, group Masses, and other special occasions. The lead-coordinator for the music ministry group selects appropriate songs compatible with the theme of the meetings, arranges for the words of the song on a viewgraph, song sheets or books, and schedules music ministry practice times. Music is provided by vocalists, flutists, guitarists, and other suitable instrumental accompaniment.

Tape Ministry
One or more members coordinate the loan-out tape library which provides taped cassettes of program talks for participants who may have missed a meeting. The tape ministry coordinator reminds borrowers to return overdue tapes and arranges for replacement of damaged or lost tapes. As the program grows and matures, the tape ministry obtains additional enrichment talks to augment their existing library. Program fees sustain initial purchase of taped talks used in program meetings. A donation of 25 cents per tape for each week borrowed helps to sustain the expenses incurred in maintaining and developing the tape library.

Book Ministry
The book ministry obtains copies of the suggested resource books as well as any additional enrichment books as part of its developing Scripture library. Books are made available at each meeting for members to preview prior to personal purchase. We have usually operated

the book ministry on a prepaid basis, purchasing the books from local religious book stores and making delivery at the beginning or end of each meeting. Program fees sustain the initial purchase of resource and enrichment reference books for the book ministry. Thereafter, the ministry becomes self-sustaining through the participant's regular book purchases.

Parish Publicity Coordinator

One coordinator is required for each parish represented in the program. The coordinator provides publicity within his/her own parish, utilizing bulletin notices, posters, newsletters, etc. . . . The coordinator acts as a contact person within the parish and provides information for his/her own parishioners concerning the Scripture Program.

Youth Ministry

The youth ministry are table discussion leader teams dedicated to groups of teens or young single adults who wish to participate within the adult parish Scripture Program at a youth table.

Baby-Sitting Coordinator

One or more coordinators arrange for mature and reliable baby-sitters during daytime meetings. Facilities, special arrangements (refreshments, name-tags or name-shirts for children, toys and baby furniture, etc.), are coordinated for the baby-sitters and mothers leaving their children. We found a dollar donation per child (maximum of two dollars per mother) or a dollar and a half donation per mother (regardless of number of children) were both satisfactory financial arrangements for the baby-sitters. Arrangements for one adult baby-sitter per eight to ten children are set up through program pre-registration.

In Event of Coordinator's Absence

In the event of absence, coordinators are encouraged to arrange for their own substitution by contacting another coordinator or member of the program; and always to inform the program leaders of the change. The importance of each job or ministry being covered at each meeting cannot be overemphasized! A list of the names, phone numbers and addresses of members assuming responsible roles is provided for all job and ministry coordinators and discussion leaders, by the program leaders.

The importance of delegating responsibilities for these supporting activities cannot be over-stressed. The program leaders will always be fully occupied leading the meetings. Responsible coordinators efficiently performing their assigned tasks can make even the largest parish or area meeting run smoothly with a minimum of difficulties.

APPENDIX D
(Name of Your) SCRIPTURE PROGRAM

TABLE-NAME _____

SERIES III—(Title & Span Time,
i.e., Feb.–May, 19xx)

FEE PAID	NAME - STREET ADDRESS - CITY	PHONE NO.	MEETING DATES - ATTENDANCE
	1. TEAM LEADER		
	2. TEAM LEADER		
	3. TEAM LEADER		
	4. TEAM LEADER		
	5. TEAM LEADER		
	6. TEAM LEADER		
	7. TEAM LEADER		
	8. TEAM LEADER		
	9. TEAM LEADER		
	10. TEAM LEADER		

APPENDIX E
WELCOME TO SAN GABRIEL VALLEY DAYTIME SCRIPTURE PROGRAM

The name of the table-group you are joining is

_____

Your team discussion leaders and their phone numbers are:

_____ ( ) _____ .

_____ ( ) _____ .

Please feel free to call them between meetings if any questions or needs arise regarding your participation in the Scripture Program. In the case of your absence one of the discussion leaders will keep any reading guides or other handouts distributed at the missed meeting, for you upon your return. They will also try to contact you to pass on pertinent home-reading information. In the event they miss you, please feel free to contact them for the information.

The weekly daytime meetings are held on Tuesday, 9:30 A.M. to Noon at Our Lady of Guadalupe Parish Hall in Irwindale. Babysitting arrangements are available (one dollar donation per child per meeting)—contact Babysitting Coordinator: _____ (name & phone no.).

The fees for program participants are $3.00 for each Series, and will be collected during the first couple of meetings of each series. The second-year program schedule will be:

Series I—Sept. 19, 1978 to Dec. 12, 1978—*The Gospel of Luke* presented by Father John Kesterson, SS.CC.

Series II—Jan. 2, 1979 to Feb. 6, 1979—*The Psalms, School of Prayer* presented by Fr. George Montague, S.M., (tapes)

Series III—Feb. 13 to May 1, 1979—*The Acts of Apostles & St. Paul* presented by Fr. Finbar Devine, SS.CC.

EXPLANATION OF SCRIPTURE PROGRAM FORMAT

During recent years it has become increasingly evident that there is a growing desire within God's people to enter more into the study of Scripture. An outgrowth of this desire for solid Catholic teaching is the longing to share with another how the words of Scripture speak to us in our daily living. Also evident is the desire to grow in our relationship with God through learning to pray with Scripture.

In the Los Angeles area a very simple Scripture Program has been in operation both in homes and at parish levels for several years. This is the second year for the area-wide Valley program. The *PURPOSE* of the Scripture Program is four-fold:

(1) To provide an opportunity to deepen our understanding and knowledge of Scripture through good Catholic teachings provided by qualified speakers, scholarly taped talks, films or filmstrips, and recommended home reading.

(2) To provide the catalyst within small group sharing that enables participants to find the application of the words of Scripture to their daily lives and to build up a spirit of Christian Community within their sharing groups.

(3) To provide the opportunity for small group praying of Scripture that contributes to the growth of the individual's personal relationship with Jesus Christ.

(4) To encourage participants to "go forth—spreading the Good News" with renewed love, concern and service to their families, parishes and communities.

The program format consists of a three-phased meeting wherein participants **study, share and pray Scripture in small groups**. The development of this format has evolved out of the expressed needs and desires of the participants. Our experience has been that this combined threefold approach of study, small group sharing and praying is the catalyst that frees the participants to experience the fruits of authentic religious adult education in their everyday lives! Such religious education is much more than an informational head trip, rather, it touches the whole person, mind and heart, intellect and attitudes, and totally molds our lives as Christians.

The knowledge that comes from solid input and the opportunity for either quiet personal reflection or group reflections through faith-sharing and discussion, helps us to identify with the knowledge received. This identification enables us to assimilate that part of the knowledge that resonates within our own life situations—an experience of renewed and deepened faith. The assimilation draws forth a personal faith-response (letting the head knowledge become heart knowledge—"putting on the mind of Jesus Christ"). Our prayer motivates us to begin to live out of what we are learning and experiencing as God's Word gradually affects our life-responses and educates our attitudes as maturing Christians.

A typical meeting begins with an hour "input" by means of a speaker or taped-talk presentation, augmented by the members' prior home reading. This is the **STUDY phase** of the meeting.

The following forty-five minutes is devoted to shared discussions within small discussion groups of up to ten persons seated around tables and assisted by a team of discussion leader/facilitators. The subject matter of the study-presentation provides material for discussion about its biblical meaning (literary, historical, theological and spiritual) as well as its personal application in individual lives. This is the **SHARING phase** of the meeting.

The last half hour is a form of extemporaneous Scripture praying on a passage compatible with the theme of the **STUDY phase** of the meeting. Following brief introductory comments the passage is read to the entire assembly; a minute or two of reflective silence follows the reading and then the individuals within each sharing group express how the passage personally has spoken to them in their lives. The passage is read a second time, again followed by a reflective silence and again personally shared within each group. After the third reading of the passage and silent reflection, the participants begin to formulate verbal prayers based upon the passage, in prayers of petition, thanksgiving, praise, etc. This is the **PRAYING SCRIPTURE phase** of the meeting.

APPENDIX F
YEAR-END EVALUATION

SAN GABRIEL VALLEY SCRIPTURE PROGRAM
SEPTEMBER, 1977 — MAY, 1978

What about the Scripture Program have you found **MOST** beneficial personally?

What about the Scripture Program have you found **LEAST** beneficial personally?

Please evaluate each phase of the Program Meetings with the application of a scale from 4 to 1 (4—Outstanding, 3—Good, 2—Fair, 1—Poor). Personal comments are also welcome.

	Eval. Number	Comments
STUDY Phase		
Taped Talks		
Guest Speakers		
Development of Theme		
Suggested Home Reading Guides—Personal Usefulness		
Scripture-Prayer-Passages Use		
Questions for Home-Study		
Books Suggested for Study		
Extra Enrichment Handouts		
SHARING Phase		
Leadership/Facilitators		
Usefulness of Discussion Questions		
Community Growth & Unity Experienced Within Table-Group		
(If not experienced—can you explain why?)		
Personal Enrichment Experienced Through Small Group Sharing		
Group-Summaries		
PRAYING SCRIPTURE Phase		
Introduction of Passage by Program Leaders		

	Eval. Number	Comments
Relevancy of Passage for Personal Application		
Community Growth through Praying Scripture Together		
Personal Growth Experienced through Scripture Prayer		
ORGANIZATION ASPECTS & PROGRAM LEADERSHIP		
Program Organization		
Leadership by Program Leaders		
Coordination & Efficiency of		
Refreshments		
Hall Set-Up & Clean-Up		
Tape Loan-Out Ministry		
Book Ministry		
Music Ministry		
Babysitting		

Suggestions for Improvement of future Scripture Programs:

What Scripture Themes or Books of the Bible would you be interested in for future programs?

Will you be registering for the next year San Gabriel Valley Scripture Program? _____ Weekly Daytime Program? _____ Twice Monthly Nighttime Program? _____

Please share with us your evaluation of the benefit you've personally experienced in your life as a result of participating in the San Gabriel Valley Scripture Program. Thank you.

Optional . . .

Name _____ Table-Group Name? _____

Your Home Parish? _____ City? _____

APPENDIX G
FIRST-YEAR SCRIPTURE
PROGRAM HOME READING GUIDES

SERIES I—OVERVIEW OF THE GREAT THEMES OF THE OLD TESTAMENT

Meeting #1 *Explanation of Program Format—Study, Share & Pray: & Get Acquainted Meeting*
by Program Leader-Couple/Team

Meeting #2 *The Call—Introduction to the Word*
by Fr. Richard Rohr, O.F.M.

Meeting #3 *Praying Scripture*
by Msgr. David Rosage, S.J.

Meeting #4 *Exodus—The Journey of Faith*
by Fr. Richard Rohr, O.F.M.

Meeting #5 *Joshua to Kings—Ordinary Becomes Extraordinary*
by Fr. Richard Rohr, O.F.M.

Meeting #6 *The Prophets—Radical Traditionists*
by Fr. Richard Rohr, O.F.M.

Meeting #7 *Genesis—God and Man*
by Fr. Richard Rohr, O.F.M.

Meeting #8 *Job—Good and Evil*
by Fr. Richard Rohr, O.F.M.

Meeting #9 *Salvation History—Faith in Evolution*
by Fr. Richard Rohr, O.F.M.

SERIES I—OVERVIEW OF THE GREAT THEMES OF THE OLD TESTAMENT

Meeting #1 (a)

Opening Prayer, Welcome and Introduction of Table Discussion Leader-Teams by Program Leaders

Biblical Table Names and Reasons Chosen Shared by Discussion Leaders with their Table Groups

Table Groups' Get Acquainted—Group-Dynamic "Diad" by Members within each Table Group

Explanation of the Purpose and Format of the Program: Study, Share and Pray Scripture by Program Leaders

SHARING Phase *among Table Groups, Using Suggested Questions*

SUGGESTED DISCUSSION/SHARING QUESTIONS

1. "Who do you say I Am" in your life? (Matthew 16:15)
(Participants are requested to write out their personal answer to this question. Then proceed int group sharing with the following questions.)

2. How was the Bible shared in your family as you grew up?

3. When did you begin to read Scripture? What was your initial response?

4. What are you hoping to receive out of your participation in this Scripture Program?

5. Share your answer, if you wish, as to "Who you say, Christ IS, today in your life."

Scripture Prayer:

Explanation of Method of Praying Scripture & Introduction of Passage by Program Leaders

*The Sower and the Seed—Matthew 13:1–23

Program Announcements: Books, Home Reading Guides, etc.

Closing Prayer

*The passages suggested to use for Scripture prayer at each meeting are marked with an (*) asterisk.

SERIES I—OVERVIEW OF THE GREAT THEMES OF THE OLD TESTAMENT

Meeting #1 (b)

Opening Prayer, Welcome and Introduction of Table Discussion Leader-Teams by Program Leaders

Biblical Table-Names and Reasons Chosen Shared by Discussion Leaders with their Table Groups

Table Groups' Get Acquainted—Group-Dynamic "Diad" by Members within each Table Group

Explanation of the Purpose and Format of the Program: Study, Share and Pray Scripture by Program Leaders

SHARING Phase among Table Groups, Using Suggested Questions

SUGGESTED DISCUSSION/SHARING QUESTIONS:

1. How can my participation this year in the Scripture Program be a means in my life, of proclaiming Christ for others?
(Participants are requested to write out their personal answer to this question. Then proceed into group sharing with the following questions.)

2. What do I hope (need) to receive from others through this program participation?

3. What do I hope to personally be able to give to and for my table group companions during this program year?

4. Share your answer, if you wish, as to how your participation in the program this year can be a means in your life of proclaiming Christ for others.

Scripture Prayer:
Explanation of Method of Praying Scripture & Introduction of Passage by Program Leaders

*Spreading the Gospel—"Good News"—Philippians 1:12–24

Program Announcements: Books, Home Reading Guides, etc.

Closing Prayer

SERIES I—OVERVIEW OF THE GREAT THEMES OF THE OLD TESTAMENT

Meeting #2
The Call—Introduction to the Word by Fr. Richard Rohr, O.F.M. (tape)

SUGGESTED HOME READING

Scripture:
Foreword and Introduction in the Bible;

How to Read the Bible;

Introductory Page to the Old Testament—The Pentateuch.

Scripture Prayer:
*Emmaus Walk—Luke 24:13–32

Wedding Banquet—Matthew 22:1–14

Invitation to Receive All as Gift—Isaiah 55:1–13

Sower and the Seed—Mark 4:1–29

Commentaries/Enrichment Books:
Reading Scripture as the Word of God by George Martin
Part I—Reading Scripture (Chapters 1 through 4), pp. 1—94

Pathways in Scripture by Damasus Winzen
Introduction: Words of Eternal Life; How to Read Scripture, pp. 1–18

Vatican II—Document on Revelation

SUGGESTED DISCUSSION/SHARING QUESTIONS:

1. What does "Faith" mean to you?

2. How are we called to be spiritually semites—to think like Jews?

3. How do you understand the meaning of this verse—"The Word of God is like a two edged sword"?

4. Discuss the statements:

(a) "Scriptures are the Constitution of the Church."

(b) "God's Words are *ever new* to us today."

SERIES I—OVERVIEW OF THE GREAT THEMES OF THE OLD TESTAMENT

Meeting #3
Praying Scripture by Msgr. David Rosage, S.J. (tape)

SUGGESTED HOME READING

Scripture:
John 8:12–59
Romans 8:14–34
Romans 15:1–7
2 Timothy 3:12; 4:8

Scripture Passages:
*Zacchaeus Meets Christ—Luke 19:1–10

God Knows and Loves me as I am—Psalm 139

Renewal of Mind in Christ—Romans 12:1–21

God's Promise of Restoration—Isaiah 43:1–28

Commentaries/Enrichment Books
Reading Scripture As the Word of God by George Martin, pp. 95–166
Part II—The Word of God (Chapters 5–7)

Man Meets God by Rev. Robert Humitz, pp. 1–14

Speak Lord, Your Servant Is Listening by Msgr. David Rosage, S.J.

Discovery of Pathways in Prayer by Msgr. David Rosage, S.J.

Trumpets of Beaten Metal by Eugene LaVerdiere

Pray—An Introduction to Spiritual Life for Busy People by Rev. Richard J. Huelsman, S.J.

SUGGESTED DISCUSSION/SHARING QUESTIONS:

1. Why is it important to approach Scripture praying with faith and trust?

2. How can we best prepare ourselves to pray Scripture?

3. What are some of the personal benefits and advantages of praying Scripture regularly?

4. What is the great transformation in us that Scripture praying can cause?

SERIES I—OVERVIEW OF THE GREAT THEMES OF THE OLD TESTAMENT

Meeting #4
Exodus—A Journey of Faith by Fr. Richard Rohr, O.F.M. (tape)

SUGGESTED HOME READING

Scripture:
Exodus 1–34
Deuteronomy 4–8, 34
Joshua 24:1–28
Hebrews 3:1–10:39

Scripture Prayer:
God's Presence in His Commandments—Deuteronomy 8:1–20

*Intimacy of a Friend with God—Exodus 33:7–23

The Past as Example to us in the Present—1 Corinthians 10:1–13

The "Exodus" Experience Seen in the "Our Father"—Matthew 6:5–15

Commentaries/Enrichment Books
Reading Scripture as the Word of God by George Martin
Parts I and II completed.

Pathways in Scripture by Damasus Winzen, O.S.B., pp. 37–85

Book of Exodus
Book of Deuteronomy
Book of Leviticus
Book of Numbers

Man Meets God by Rev. Robert Humitz, pp. 15–30
Unit II, Sections 1 through 4—Meaning of Exodus Experience

SUGGESTED DISCUSSION/SHARING QUESTIONS:

1. Discuss meaning and purpose of the "desert experience" for the Israelites? For you today?

2. How does God teach His People to depend upon Him?

3. What kind of "idols" do we set up for ourselves today?

4. How have I experienced God's faithfulness? (Gift of "Hindsight")

5. Discuss the meaning of the statement: "Faith is the security to be insecure."

6. How is *your* "carpet" today?

SERIES I—OVERVIEW OF THE GREAT THEMES OF THE OLD TESTAMENT

Meeting #5
Joshua to Kings—Ordinary Becomes Extraordinary by Fr. Richard Rohr, O.F.M. (tape)

*This tape is longest of series—could be split in half so this meeting material would take two meetings.

SUGGESTED HOME READING

Scripture:
Joshua 1–4, 24
Judges 2:6–3:6, 6–8
1 Samuel 8–9, 16–20, 29–31
2 Samuel 6–7, 11–12, 25
1 Kings 5–6, 11–12, 17–20, 22
2 Kings 2–9

Scripture Passages:
God's Promise to David—2 Samuel 7:8–29

Elisha's Walk in Faith—2 Kings 2:1–15

*The Psychology of God with Elijah—1 Kings 19:3–16

Expectant Faith of Elijah—1 Kings 17:7–24 & 2 Kings 4:42–44

Commentaries/Enrichment Books:
Pathways in Scripture by Damasus Winzen, O.S.B., pp. 87–138

Book of Joshua
Book of Judges
Book of Kings
Book of 1 and 2 Samuel

Man Meets God by Rev. Robert Humitz, pp. 31–44

Unit III, Section 1 through 3—Land of Promise, Reign of David, and the Divided Kingdom

SUGGESTED DISCUSSION/SHARING QUESTIONS:

1. What were some of the ways the Israelites saw God teaching them to trust in him?

2. In what ways do we put our trust in "lesser gods"? What are my "lesser gods"?

3. In what ways do I prevent "God from being God for me"?

4. How can I become a "child" before God?

5. What is meant by the phrase "God has no grandchildren"?

6. Discuss the phrase, "Wherever your mind goes when your mind is free—that is where your heart is!"

SERIES I—OVERVIEW OF THE GREAT THEMES OF THE OLD TESTAMENT

Meeting #6
The Prophets—Radical Traditionists by Fr. Richard Rohr, O.F.M. (tape)

SUGGESTED HOME READING

Scripture:
Nehemiah 8–10
Isaiah 1, 6–12
Isaiah 40–55 (Book II)
Isaiah 56–66 (Book III)

Scripture Passages:
Vineyard of God in Prophecy and Parable—Isaiah 5:1–7 and Matthew 21:33–45

Messianic Prophecy & Fulfillment—Isaiah 42:1–9 and Matthew 12:16–21

*Invitation to Grace—Isaiah 55:1–13

Promises of Redemption & Restoration—Isaiah 43:1–28

The Servant of the Lord—Isaiah 49:1–27

Commentaries/Enrichment Books:
Pathways in Scripture by Damasus Winzen, O.S.B., pp. 195–204

Prophecy of Isaiah
Prophecy of Jeremiah
Prophecy of Ezekiel
Prophecy of Minor Prophets

Man Meets God by Rev. Robert Humitz, pp. 52–53

Unit IV, Section 2—Remnant Carried Into Captivity

These Stones Will Shout by Rev. Mark Link, S.J.

The Men and the Message of the Old Testament by Rev. Peter Ellis, C.SS.R.

Listen, Prophets! by George Maloney, S.J.

SUGGESTED DISCUSSION/SHARING QUESTIONS:

1. What was/is the role of a prophet as revealed biblically?

2. Why were the prophets usually rejected? What usually happened to them?

3. Discuss the differences between the institutional and charismatic men of the Old Testament.

4. Is there a Prophet you can personally relate to in your life? Who? Explain why?

5. How are we called to be "prophets" today? What may be the cost?

SERIES I—OVERVIEW OF THE GREAT THEMES OF THE OLD TESTAMENT

Meeting #7
Genesis—God and Man by Rev. Richard Rohr, O.F.M. (tape—1st half)

SUGGESTED HOME READING

Scripture:
Genesis 1–12
Hebrews 11:1–40
Romans 4:1–5:22

Daniel 3:52–90
Genesis 13–50

Scripture Passages:
Creation—It is Good!—Genesis 1:1–23 and 2:4–25

In Praise of Creation—Psalm 8 and Psalm 104

Call & Covenant of Abraham—Genesis 12:1–19 and 15:1–21

*Our inheritance by Faith—Romans 4:13–5:5

Jesus' Obedience Unto Death—Philippians 2:1–11

Commentaries/Enrichment Books:
Pathways in Scripture by Rev. Damasus Winzen, O.S.B.

Genesis 1–11—Primeval History
Genesis 12–50—The Patriarchal Period

Man Meets God by Rev. Robert Humitz, pp. 63–65

Unit V, Section 1—A Return to the Beginnings

Two-Edged Sword by Rev. John McKenzie, S.J.

ACTA Foundation Scripture Commentary—#1—Penteteuch

Liturgical Press O.T. Reading Guides #4—Genesis 12–50, #9—Genesis 1–11

SUGGESTED DISCUSSION/SHARING QUESTIONS:

1. What was the purpose of writing Genesis? For the Israelites? For us today?

2. Discuss the meaning—"we are all children of Abraham, whether Jew, Moslem or Christian."

3. What is meant by "Biblical Religion"? "Biblical Faith"? How do they apply to our lives today?

4. What is God's answer to man's problems? How do you experience his answer to your needs?

5. Share/discuss your understanding of personally "walking with God."

SERIES I—OVERVIEW OF THE GREAT THEMES OF THE OLD TESTAMENT

Meeting #8
Job—Good and Evil by Rev. Richard Rohr, O.F.M. (tape—last half)

SUGGESTED HOME READING

Scripture:
Book of Job

Scripture Passages:
Knowledge of the "Heart" and Job's Restoration—Job 42:1–10

Letting Go—Letting God Lead One's Life—Philippians 3:7–16

*The Trials and Hope of the Apostolate—2 Corinthians 4:5–18

To Suffer with Christ Is To Be Glorified with Christ—Romans 8:14–27

Endurance in Midst of Trials—James 1:2–7, 12–25

Commentaries/Enrichment Books:
Pathways in Scripture by Rev. Damasus Winzen, pp. 161–173

The Book of Job

Man Meets God by Rev. Robert Humitz, pp. 66–67

Unit V, Section 2—The Wisdom Literature of Israel

ACTA Foundation Scripture Commentary—#6—Wisdom

Liturgical Press O.T. Reading Guide #27—Job, Qoheleth

SUGGESTED DISCUSSION/SHARING QUESTIONS:

1. What is the meaning of the Book of Job? For the Israelites? For us today?

2. Where do we find "Job's friends" today? Discuss how they affect us in our times of sufferings.

3. What do you think of how Job talked to God? Could you do the same?

4. What is the meaning/message in God's answer to Job's complaints?

5. What is your understanding of the phrase, "I am God, you are man"?

6. Have you personally found meaning through the sufferings you've experienced? Would you like to share?

SERIES I—OVERVIEW OF THE GREAT THEMES OF THE OLD TESTAMENT

Meeting #9
Salvation History—The Evolution of Faith by Rev. Richard Rohr, O.F.M. (tape)

SUGGESTED HOME READING

Scripture:
Book of Daniel

Scripture Passages:
*Promise of Redemption and Restoration—Isaiah 43:1–28

God's Goodness Despite Israel's Ingratitude—Psalm 78

Trust in the Lord—Psalm 27

The Miserere: Prayer of Repentance—Psalm 51

Desire for the Sanctuary of God—Psalm 84

How Personal and Total God's Love is for each Person—Psalm 139

Commentaries/Enrichment Books:
Pathways in Scripture by Rev. Damasus Winzen, pp. 173–184, 223–226

Book of Psalms   The Prophecy of Daniel

Man Meets God by Rev. Robert Humitz, pp. 69–73

Unit VI—Hope for Intervention of Yahweh

Face to Face with God—The Biblical Way to Pray by Rev. Jacques Loew

Thirsting for the Lord—Essays in Biblical Spirituality by Rev. Carroll Stuhlmueller, C.P.

SUGGESTED DISCUSSION/SHARING QUESTIONS:

1. What was the "faith-evolution" of the Israelites?

2. How are we, as the Church, or you personally, like Israel in our relationship with God? Discuss the Church's "faith-evolution."

3. Discuss—"It is much easier to believe ideas than to love God personally."

4. What is the meaning of the statement—"Man becomes the 'God' he worships"?

5. Why is it necessary for us personally to come to an *experiential* knowledge of God in our individual lives?

6. Would you like to share your personal experience of "salvation history" as experienced in your life?

FIRST-YEAR SCRIPTURE PROGRAM SERIES II—OVERVIEW OF THE GREAT THEMES OF THE NEW TESTAMENT

Meeting #1 *Matthew's Good News—The Reign of God*
by Rev. Richard Rohr, O.F.M.

Meeting #2 *Mark and John—Jesus Is Lord*
by Rev. Richard Rohr, O.F.M.

Meeting #3 *Luke and Acts —A New Life*
by Rev. Richard Rohr, O.F.M.

Meeting #4 *Mary, Prayer and the Church*
by Rev. Richard Rohr, O.F.M.

Meeting #5 *Paul—A Life In Christ*
by Rev. Richard Rohr, O.F.M.

Meeting #6 *Apocalypse—The New Creation*
by Rev. Richard Rohr, O.F.M.

Meeting #7 *Holy Land Slide Presentation and Sharing of Trip*
by Guest Speaker or Program Member
*Celebration of Eucharist—Thanksgiving for Year
Concluding with Potluck Lunch (Dinner or Dessert)*

SERIES II—OVERVIEW OF GREAT THEMES OF THE NEW TESTAMENT

Meeting #1
Matthew's Good News —The Reign of God by Rev. Richard Rohr, O.F.M. (tape)

SUGGESTED HOME READING

Scripture:
Gospel according to Matthew

Scripture Passages:
NOW-experience description of Christian Living—Matthew 5:3–12

Christian Forgiveness and Retribution—Matthew 5:23–28, 38–48

*Christ Calls Matthew to "Follow"—Matthew 9:9–13

Jesus Asks, "Who Do You Say That I Am?"—Matthew 16:13–20

Jesus Tells Us of His Father's Love—Matthew 11:25–30

Christ's Commission of the Apostles—Matthew 28:16–20

Commentary/Enrichment Books
Man Meets God by Rev. Robert Humitz, pp. 75–88

Unit VII, Section 1–3—Jesus, Fulfillment of Hopes of Israel

Who Do You Say That I Am? by Rev. Edward Ciuba, pp. 1–46, 101–126

Foreword and Chapters 1–3 and 7

Invitation to Matthew—Commentary by Rev. Donald Senior

Gospel of St. Matthew—Read and Pray Series by Rev. Donald Senior

SUGGESTED DISCUSSION/SHARING QUESTIONS:

1. Why did Matthew write his Gospel? For whom? What was his message?

2. What does discipleship mean, as revealed in Jesus' relationship with others in the Gospel stories?

3. Discuss—how we are called to be Jesus' disciples today?

4. Discuss what this statement means to you—"My Faith is the present-experience of the Lord Jesus in my life".

5. Do the Beatitudes, as descriptions of relationships, speak to your NOW-experience of Christian living? If so, which ones? Explain in what ways they apply.

6. Discuss who are people living today who are exemplars of Living-a-Beatitude by their way/attitude of life.

SERIES II—OVERVIEW OF THE GREAT THEMES OF THE NEW TESTAMENT

Meeting #2
Mark and John—Jesus Is Lord by Rev. Richard Rohr, O.F.M. (tape)

SUGGESTED HOME READING

Scripture:
Gospel of Mark					Gospel of John

Scripture Passages:
*The Disciple's Love—John 15:9–17

All Believers—John 17:20–23

Love For One Another—John 13:34–35

Faith, Hope and Love—Romans 5:1–11

Commentaries/Enrichment Books:
Pathways in Scripture by Rev. Damasus Winzen, pp. 230–250, 263–274

Gospel of Mark					Gospel of John

Who Do You Say That I Am? by Rev. Edward Ciuba, pp. 79–100

Chapter VII—Miracles: Signs of the Kingdom

Gospel of St. John—Read and Pray Series by Pheme Perkins

Maranatha—Reflection on the Mystical Theology of St. John by Rev. William J. Fulco, S.J.

SUGGESTED DISCUSSION/SHARING QUESTIONS:

1. Why was John the Baptist's call to repent, reform and renewal preparing the way for Christ? How do we hear similar "calls" today in the Church? In our own lives?

2. Discuss the phrase, "Christianity is not attending a meeting; Christianity is sharing life!"

3. Why are the qualities of forgiveness and love essential to living a Christ-centered life? For interpersonal relationships? For community-life?

4. Discuss why and how the quality of our interpersonal relationships reflects and reveals the maturity of our relationship in the Spirit with Christ.

5. Share your personal experience of the truth of Fr. Rohr's statement: "I know who God Is by how He relates to His people! I know Jesus by His people who have given their lives over to Him! They witness His Life and Truth to me!"

SERIES II—OVERVIEW OF THE GREAT THEMES OF THE NEW TESTAMENT

Meeting #3
Luke and Acts—A New Gift by Rev. Richard Rohr, O.F.M. (tape)

SUGGESTED HOME READING

Scripture:
Gospel of Luke					Acts of the Apostles

Scripture Passages:
*The Good Samaritan—Luke 10:25–37

A Lesson in Humility—Luke 14:7–24

The Holy Eucharist Is Gift—Luke 22:14–20

Promise and Gift of the Holy Spirit—Acts 1:6–9, 12–14; 2:1–4, 14–18, 32–33

Gift of Community Life—Acts 2:42–47

"What Must I Do To Be Saved?"—Acts 16:25–34

Commentaries/Enrichment Books:
Pathways in Scripture by Rev. Damasus Winzen, pp. 251–262, 275–284

Gospel of Luke   Acts of the Apostles

Man Meets God by Rev. Robert Humitz, pp. 121–126

Unit IX, Section 1—The Early Church.

Who Do You Say That I Am? by Rev. Edward Ciuba, pp. 47–62, 127–144

Chapter IV and VIII

Invitation to Luke—Commentary by Rev. Robert J. Karris

Gospel of St. Luke—Read and Pray Series by Rev. Robert J. Karris

SUGGESTED DISCUSSION/SHARING QUESTIONS:

1. Describe the early Church's experience of "Community." Describe the early Christian Community's experience of "Church."

2. Where and/or how do we experience similar "Community" today?

3. What is the "Good News" that Christ came to give to us?

4. How can we "go spread the 'Good News' " to others? Share practical everyday examples you've experienced in your life or seen in the lives of others that revealed the "Good News" of Christ to another.

5. Why will a true Christian today be a "sign of contradiction to the world"? In what ways? How do you feel about being such a Christian?

6. Discuss—"People are liberated in a life time, it is a growing process, not a 'zap' instant!"

SERIES II—OVERVIEW OF THE GREAT THEMES OF THE NEW TESTAMENT

Meeting #4
Mary, Prayer and the Church by Rev. Richard Rohr, O.F.M. (tape)

SUGGESTED HOME READING

Scripture:
Matthew 1:18–24 and 2:1–23   John 19:25–30
Luke 1:26–80 and 2:1–52

Scripture Passages:
The Birth of Jesus—Matthew 1:18–25

The Annunciation—Luke 1:34–35

Elizabeth's Proclamation—Luke 1:42–44

*Wedding at Cana—John 2:1–12

"There Is Your Mother"—John 19:26–27

Commentaries/Enrichment Books:
Pathways in Scripture by Damasus Winzen, O.S.B., pp. 254–259

Gospel of Luke (section on Mary)

Mary, The Womb of God by George Maloney, S.J.

The Glory of Israel (Mysteries of the Rosary in Scripture) by Ronald Wallis, pp. 13–36

Scriptural Rosary (Modern Version of Praying the Rosary with Scripture)

SUGGESTED DISCUSSION/SHARING QUESTIONS:

1. What was the importance of Mary's role in God's salvation?

2. What occurs at Calvary when Jesus gives his Mother to the Beloved Disciple?

3. What are some typically feminine traits that are helpful in disposing ourselves to God?

4. Discuss the phrase, "Prayer is a *being* for another, not necessarily a *doing*."

5. What do you feel is a proper devotion to Mary?

SERIES II—OVERVIEW OF THE GREAT THEMES OF THE NEW TESTAMENT

Meeting #5
Paul—A New Life in Christ by Rev. Richard Rohr, O.F.M. (tape)

SUGGESTED HOME READING

Scripture:
Epistles to Philippians, Ephesians and Colossians

Scripture Passages:
Christian Dedication—Philippians 3:7–16

*Unity in the Mystical Body—Ephesians 4:1–7, 11–16

Renewal in Christ—Ephesians 4:17–24

The Practice of Virtue—Colossians 3:12–21

Commentaries/Enrichment Books:
Pathways in Scripture by Rev. Damasus Winzen, pp. 285–310

Letters of St. Paul   The Seven Catholic Letters

Man Meets God by Rev. Robert Humitz, pp. 130–136

Unit IX, Section 3—Paul Lives In Christ

Jesus Is Lord: Paul's Life In Christ by Joseph Blenkinsopp

Building Christ's Body—The Dynamics of Christian Living According to Paul by Rev. George Montague, S.M.

SUGGESTED DISCUSSION/SHARING QUESTIONS:

1. Paul shared his new life in Christ by his presence and by his letters. Discuss how God calls us to share ourselves with one another for his sake.

2. Discuss the statement: "Church is not just attending a function, Church is relationships between people."

3. How is hospitality God's gift for others? Describe a Christian-hospitable person's attitude.

4. What is your response to the statement—"Unless I am an impossible sign to the world, I am not a sign at all"? What does it mean to you?

5. Why are "cozy communities" usually an end in themselves?

6. How do you experience being called daily to a "new life in Christ"? Would you like to share your experience of living a "new life in Christ"?

SERIES II—OVERVIEW OF THE GREAT THEMES OF THE NEW TESTAMENT

Meeting #6
Apocalypse—The New Creation by Rev. Richard Rohr, O.F.M. (tape)

SUGGESTED HOME READING

Scripture:
Book of Revelation

Scripture Passages:
*Letter to Laodicea—Revelation 3:14–22

Triumph of the Elect—Revelation 7:9–17

Salvation and Power—Revelation 12:10–12

New Heaven and New Earth—Revelation 21:1–7

Commentaries/Enrichment Books:
Pathways in Scripture by Rev. Damasus Winzen, pp. 311–320

Book of Apocalypse

Man Meets God by Rev. Robert Humitz, pp. 155–158

Themes of Revelation

What Did Jesus Teach About the End of the World? by Rev. Franz Mussner

The Book of Revelation, What Does It Really Say? by Rev. John Randall, S.T.D.

SUGGESTED DISCUSSION/SHARING QUESTIONS:

1. What is the biblical description of a prophet?
2. What is meant by the phrase, "Jesus is the only Thing that ever really happened in all history"?
3. What is meant by "living expectantly in the present moment"?
4. Why are people living together in community and love a sign of God's presence in the world?
5. Why was the Book of Revelations written?
6. What is the Book of Revelations' basic message for us today?

SERIES II—OVERVIEW OF THE GREAT THEMES OF THE NEW TESTAMENT

Meeting #7
Holy Land Slide Presentation and Sharing of Trip by Guest Speaker or Program Member who has been there.

This presentation lasts an hour to an hour and a half followed by

Celebration of Eucharist

in thanksgiving for the Scripture Program year together.

Conclude with a pre-planned
Potluck Lunch (or Dessert, if evening program),
by all the program participants.

Chapter 5
YOUTH MINISTRY SCRIPTURE PROGRAMS

An early awareness of the value of approaching Scriptures through the combined dynamics of study, group sharing and praying evolved when seven young people and their parents entered into a home Scripture study in September 1974. The parents, each experienced high-school catechists, took turns as team-couples in leading weekly meetings over a two-year period. Their Scripture study, sharing and praying, led them into an introductory overview of the Old and New Testament the first year, and the following year into a broad view of the Gospel of Matthew with a final series on meeting Christ in the sacraments. In the "light" of the Gospel message the parents shared their faith-experiences of Christian living with the aim toward enabling the young people to gradually enter into a more personal awareness of their own daily experiences in living faith-filled Christian lives.

When the first parish Scripture Program developed in 1976, a Youth Ministry table of eleven young people with an engaged couple as discussion leaders, proved as effective as the home program had been. Within the past year additional home and parish Scripture Programs have been specifically adapted for the needs, interests and receptivity of the young people. The sharing within this section are the "fruit" of the experiences these various youth Scripture groups have nurtured.

Goal
The goal of the adaptation of the study, share and pray format for youth Scripture groups is to enable young people to discover experientially *where* and *how* they can meet Jesus Christ as his "call" is personally heard in each of their lives. For many young people already "touched" by Jesus in their lives, a Scripture Program experience will deepen their relationships with him and guide them in their Christian maturation process.

The awareness of "where" is experientially provided through meetings encompassing the aspects of Scripture, Community, Prayer and Service. The experience of "how" is provided through the adaptation of the basic program format of study, sharing and praying Scripture, with the additional encouragement to evangelize by sharing their experience of the "Good News" through opportunities of Christian service in their home, parish and neighborhood communities.

Scripture
A solid foundation of scriptural understanding is received through various study approaches and techniques. The sharing and praying of Scripture in small groups is the catalyst that enables the youth to experience the reality of God's Word becoming "alive" in their personal lives. For youth to imitate and follow Jesus by living in His Spirit today, they must come to know the historical Jesus revealed in the Gospels. Jesus' attitudes and responses in His life and relationships give meaning to His words today. The study of the Scriptures reveals to the youth that Jesus is alive, yesterday, today and always!

Youth leaders should encourage the young people to acquire their own personal Bible and bring it to every meeting. Paperback Bibles should be made available for the young people who do not have a Bible. It is also helpful if all members of the group are using the same translation.

Community
Through personal faith-sharing with their peers, the youth experience growth in mutual acceptance, trust, openness and love that creates a spirit of Christian community that is so essential for psychological and spiritual maturation. In loving interpersonal relationships within a community of believers, the members are able to experience the reality of their faith. As St. Paul described his need for the community of believers in Rome: ". . . I long to see you and share with you some spiritual gift to strengthen you . . . what I wish is that we may be mutually encouraged by our common faith" (Rom. 1:11–12).

The youth leaders' openness to and acceptance of the young people at their point of need will exemplify how Jesus also loves and cares for them personally. Community-building is an important aspect of each meeting. Leaders should also strive to provide the necessary means (comfortable place, music, refreshments, etc.), that will be conducive to a warm and welcoming environment.

Prayer
Just as personal sharing and communication form the "life-line" of loving relationships that create Christian community; so also is prayer the spiritual "life-line" of sharing and listening that leads the youth into a deeper relationship with Jesus Christ. We talk about praying and our children are taught their prayers; but too often our youth do not really know how to pray! Gently, lovingly and simply, faith-filled team leaders must share their prayer-life with the youth and lead them into the experience of personal and shared prayer within the community. Scripture prayer teaches youth not only how to speak to God in all situations of life, but also how to listen to the multiple ways God speaks to them as well.

Service

When the experience of meeting Jesus Christ through Scripture, community and prayer is authentic, it must be shared! "Shout joyfully to God, all you on earth, sing praise to the glory of his name; proclaim his glorious praise" (Ps. 66:1). Christian evangelization and service are essentially the way Christ-centered persons live and share what they believe and experience as Truth in their lives. Team leaders should guide and encourage youth into the experience of "living their faith" through helping them search out ways of sharing with and serving others. "They need to be encouraged to make the Gospel of 'love your neighbor as yourself' a reality in their lives" ("Ministry and Social Justice" from Youth Ministry Guidelines for Archdiocese of Los Angeles).

There are levels of Christian service to which team leaders need to be sensitive for the guidance of the young people. Evangelization is not so much talking about Jesus as it is talking *like* Jesus! Therefore the first level of service and evangelization is to encourage the youth to *let* Jesus love and serve them personally through changing their attitudes and responses in their interpersonal relationships and life situations so they can come more in line with His attitudes and responses as revealed in the Gospels.

As the youth are encouraged to let Jesus serve them in helping them find their self-identities in relationship to Him, they will also become open to broader areas of Christian service. With the maturing of their Christ-centered attitudes, the youth will usually experience a willingness and desire to serve others. Such service is often as nitty-gritty practical as was Jesus' washing the feet of his apostles. Youth Ministry leaders should solicit suggestions from the youth and look for service opportunities to suggest for individual and group service actions. It is good to remind the young people that just as Jesus began with his "own," their Christian service and evangelization should always begin "at home" and then move out into the community of all of God's people. Time should be allowed at the beginning or end of each meeting for individual reports or "witnessing" concerning activities of service and evangelization.

Through the enlightenment of Scripture study, supported by the community spirit, strengthened through shared prayer, the youth leaders aim to lead the youth into the ongoing experience of living the reality of Jesus' words: "what I just did was to give you an example: as I have done, so you must do" (Jn. 13:15). ". . . this is my Commandment: love one another as I have loved you" (Jn. 15:12).

HOW TO ORGANIZE AND SET UP A YOUTH SCRIPTURE GROUP

The approach to organizing a youth ministry Scripture group will always depend upon the interests and circumstances of the youth ministry catechists, the leaders and the young people who will participate in the program.

Within an established parish high-school religious education program (Confraternity of Christian Doctrine) one of the class electives offered during a semester can be a Bible study adapted to the format of study, sharing and praying Scripture. Parishes with youth ministry programs can easily include a Scripture group into their concept of "interweaving" teachings and activities. The organizational approach we will present in this section will be generally geared toward the establishment of a youth Scripture group as an elective within a parish's high-school C.C.D. or youth ministry program.

Other approaches that will be detailed later in this chapter under alternative structures and study approaches include:

1. Youth Scripture Programs conducted by several families wherein the parents and their teenagers form a community that studies, shares and prays Scripture together.

2. A youth Serendipity Scripture group adapted for a family-shared experience involving all age-level members of the family.

3. A youth ministry table group participating in an adult parish Scripture Program.

4. Area youth Scripture Programs as follow-up of regularly scheduled Christian (youth) concerts.

To begin a youth Scripture group within the existing structure of the parish high-school C.C.D. or youth ministry program, a few general guidelines must be considered.

Team leadership is always preferable for the same reasons given in the adult Scripture Program. Either one or both leaders should be qualified high-school or youth ministry catechists with training and experience in understanding the emotional and psychological needs of young people.

Young people who have expressed an interest in the establishment of a youth Scripture group should be asked to the initial planning meetings. Their input will contribute to the program leaders' understanding of the youth's emotional and psychological needs and areas of interest in Scripture studies.

The leader team is responsible for the selection of the biblical themes, resources, study and prayer approaches (which may include special techniques and methods), and the length of the series based on their awareness of the average age-level, background and scriptural exposure of the young people.

A comfortable meeting place is arranged by the team leaders, preferably a (home) living room or (church) lounge. If a classroom or hall with tables and chairs must be used, it should be set up in a conversational circle where each member can see and hear the other members. The meeting place and seating arrangements are an important factor in creating an open, relaxed, non-classroom environment that will encourage participation rather than a spectator-observer response.

Each program group should not exceed twelve to fifteen members, including the team leaders. Eight to ten members is ideal for good participation. If more than one youth Scripture group is established, it is preferable and often more effective, if they can meet separately in different locations. This allows for greater flexibility in moving from one phase of the meeting to another, and also allows the leaders and program members to be more sensitive to the specific areas of interest and activity of their particular group.

Where a large youth Scripture Program is planned in a common meeting area, the small table groupings of eight to ten members including the team discussion leaders should be arranged. As in the parish size (adult) programs, the study input is then presented to the entire assembly, while the sharing and praying of Scripture is done within the small sharing groups.

Reports and "witnessing" on individual service projects are suitable for the small groupings, while the overall group service projects should be shared with the full assembly during a time of general reporting. Periodic personal witnessing by individual members before the whole group, especially suitable at the closing liturgies of a series, are also extremely effective times of peer evangelization.

Although we have experienced good interaction and response from a varied age group (12 years through 20 years of age) within a single table group, it is preferable in a parish structure to divide the young people into relatable age groups. Junior-high and high-school freshmen and sophomores will usually respond more enthusiastically to a variety of youth-adapted techniques of study and prayer presentations. As they mature in their love and experience with God's Word, they can be challenged to a more direct study approach that does not depend upon attention-getting techniques. High-school juniors and seniors and young college-age adults usually adapt most comfortably to the same type of study approaches described in the home and parish (adult) Scripture Programs. As the program develops and their sense of community matures, they often prefer greater personal involvement in the study and prayer preparation, as well as in the group sharing.

Publicity

Publicity for a youth Scripture Program is equally as important as it is for adult programs. All means of publicity described in the organization of a parish program in Chapter 4, should be considered for use in publicizing the youth program. The means include parish newsletters, Sunday bulletin notices, "flyers" distributed at Sunday Masses, pulpit announcements and invitations, as well as personal one-to-one invitations by program leaders, parish priests, and the young people themselves.

When names and addresses of interested young people are available, personal letters of invitation, including an explanation of the program and a registration form, should be sent out four weeks prior to the proposed starting date. A second follow-up letter, more in the style of a "flyer," should be sent out two weeks before the starting date. The week before the program begins the team leaders should personally call each young person who has signed up in response to the publicity letters. The "word-of-mouth" publicity by parish youth leaders, priests and the young people will always be the most effective form of invitation and publicity!

Resources

The resources for Scripture study and shared prayer that are available for youth groups are exciting! There are many publishers of material geared for youth ministry programs that offer good techniques and varied study and prayer processes. Certain scriptural study guides and commentaries are specifically written for the young adult or are suitable for adaptation by the team leaders through their own teachings. Some excellent prayer-guide books have been published that are filled with a variety of "how-to" approaches such as group shared prayer, introduction into personal prayer and meditation, and variations for praying Scripture. We urge youth Scripture Program leaders to familiarize themselves with these materials, so that they know what resources are available when planning their programs. A listing of books we have found helpful in developing youth programs is included at the end of this chapter as Appendix A. A listing of publishers that specialize in material developed for the needs of youth ministry is also included as Appendix B.

The book resources are primarily for catechists' preparation, not usually for general distribution to the young people in the program. The catechist conveys the material in his/her own words, feelings and understanding as they have come to know it through individual personal study, reflection and prayer. The team leaders will find in the books listed for youth ministry, as well as in books listed in the last chapter, abundant reference material from which they can prepare their teachings. Many of the books listed for youth ministry Scripture use also have accompanying teacher manuals and are so noted on the book list.

Audio-visuals are always well received as supplementary study input for a program series. Many of the films and filmstrips listed in the third chapter under suggested themes and related resources, and in the last chapter under audio-visuals, are geared to the interests of the high-school and college-age person. Of special interest for youth ministry Scripture Programs is the ongoing development of the Genesis Project's *"New Media Bible."* These films with study guides are excellent study input. We found them especially well received by the young people at the youth ministry table when we used them in the parish (adult) Scripture Program.

The use of taped talks should be determined by the maturity of the young people and their receptivity for long periods of concentrated listening. Taped talks are most effective and usually well received by the senior-high school and college-age young adults. Younger groups usually find concentrated listening for long periods of time more difficult and therefore they may prefer not to use taped talks for their study input. The only effective exception of using taped talks with younger groups has been the selection of a brief (5 to 15 minutes) section of a talk that develops and emphasizes a specific point or theme. While team leaders may decide not to use the taped talks directly with the youth in the meetings, they should still seriously consider using them personally during their own teaching preparation or as additional background information to support a meeting theme.

In all cases, **team leaders should preview and evaluate all resource materials**, books, audio-visuals, taped talks, etc., before presenting them as study input for a youth Scripture meeting. Leaders should also **familiarize themselves with the various study techniques and prayer methods** (suggested later in this chapter) before using any of them at a meeting.

The team leaders should formulate appropriate discussion-starter questions for facilitating the **SHARING phase** of the meeting. "Head" and "heart" questions should be based on the meeting's theme, study approach and related resources.

Initially the team leaders will select the Scripture passage to be used for the **PRAYING SCRIPTURE phase** of the meeting. It should be complementary to the study-theme of the meeting. A brief introductory commentary on the background of the selected passage helps to personalize the application of the passage and is always beneficial before praying the passage. Refer to the **PRAYING SCRIPTURE phase** section of Chapter 2 for helpful attitudes and approaches when praying Scripture. Team leaders or a member of the group should always prepare the background introduction beforehand.

STRUCTURE OF A YOUTH SCRIPTURE MEETING

The structure of a youth Scripture meeting is similar to the adult home meeting insofar as the same basic format of study, sharing and praying Scripture is utilized. An added aspect of the youth meetings is the planning of actions for individual or group Christian service or evangelization, which are then reported at subsequent meetings. A further difference in the youth meetings is the variety of study techniques that are adapted from the various study approaches and resources. When youth leaders and catechists are attuned to the needs and responses of the young people, then flexibility and variety in the meetings is often most evident.

STUDY Phase

The **STUDY phase** incorporates one or more of the approaches and/or study techniques described within this chapter. There is always greater opportunity to vary the selection of study methods during a series, and the leaders should make a concentrated effort to involve the youth in some of these study techniques as often as possible. Additional study techniques are described in the *Encyclopedia of Serendipity* by Lyman Coleman, *The Mustard Seed* by Mark Link, S.J., *Pray* by Richard Huelsman, S.J. (a moderator's manual is available also), *The Bible As Drama* by Rev. Lawrence Waddy, *Bible Study Can Be Exciting!* by Mary Garvin and in the following Youth Ministry study guides: *A Journey To Emmaus: Recognizing the Lord* by Jeanne Heiberg, *To Live As Christ* series published by William Co., Brown and Co., *The Center for Learning* series published by William H. Sadlier Inc., and *The Encounter Series* published by Winston Press. The study-input time should entail approximately one-fourth of the total meeting time.

SHARING Phase

The **SHARING phase** of the meeting is always aimed at totally involving all of the young people in the group in the discussion. Certain study techniques will automatically allow the meeting to flow into the **SHARING phase** through the involvement of the youth and as they share "key" questions posed by the catechist. The youth should be encouraged to pose questions themselves and the leaders should always try to encourage a response within the group before providing an answer. The leader's familiarity with the methods of group dynamics is important in cultivating meaningful group sharing. Initially the young people may need to be encouraged to participate during the ***SHARING phase***. However, as an atmosphere of trust and openness develops, they will voluntarily become more active and spontaneously enter into the group sharing. Specific questions or statements for discussion should be prepared by the youth catechist or leader and used, if necessary, in stimulating the group sharing. The length of the ***SHARING phase*** is approximately one half of the total meeting time.

Service
Part of the time allowed for sharing should be focused on examining various possibilities of individual or group actions of Christian service or evangelization. Often the study theme and group discussions will direct the group's attention to specific needs and the kinds of actions that they will be interested in acting upon. A time should also be allowed during which the youth can report on their past service actions or opportunities of evangelization. Such a report or "witnessing" should include a description of what was done, how the action benefited another, and the personal feeling the young person experienced as a result of doing the action. Feedback from other members of the group should also be encouraged.

This service planning and sharing time may be allowed at the beginning of the meeting before the study input, during or at the end of the ***SHARING phase***, or at the end of the meeting after the praying phase. The leaders should choose where in the meeting timetable they wish to include the service planning and sharing. It is advisable to keep to a consistent pattern, so that time is always allowed for it. From five to fifteen minutes should be adequate for this activity during the meeting.

PRAYING SCRIPTURE Phase
The praying phase can utilize not only all the previously described methods of Scripture prayer used in the adult programs, but also many of the shared-prayer techniques described in prayer-resource books that are/can be geared to youth. More mature young people will usually adapt to and prefer to use the various methods of Scripture prayer outlined for the adult programs. The younger participants and those who have not had much experience with group shared-prayer will usually respond best to prayer techniques such as those described in *Experiments in Prayer* and *Experiments in Growth* by Betsy Caprio, *You* and *The Mustard Seed* by Mark Link, S.J., *Pray* by Richard Huelsman, S.J., and *Bible Study Can Be Exciting!* by Mary Garvin.

When Scripture prayer is used during the praying phase, two of the most popular methods with youth are:

1. The passage is first read slowly and prayerfully to the group, followed by silent, prayerful reflection. There is no sharing after this first reading. The passage is read a second time, followed by personal sharing of the members. After the third reading, the group prays spontaneously in their own words.

2. The passage is first read slowly and prayerfully to the group, followed by silent, prayerful reflection; there is no sharing at this time. After the second reading, the youth are encouraged to write out their reflections on the passage and its personal application in their lives. Following the third reading, they personally share either in their own words or by reading what they have written.

In both of these approaches, before the first reading, one of the youth leaders gives a brief background introduction of the passage and offers some suggestions for reflection on personal application of the passage. Various members can be asked to read each of the three readings. After the third reading and praying or sharing, the youth leader should invite the young people to join hands and verbalize any personal intentions for which they would like the group to pray. Often, if the youth leaders first express their own personal intentions, other members will also join with their needs and intentions. In this way, the young people experience first hand personally praying for the needs of others within the group and they also experience others showing their concern by praying for their needs as well. This mutual caring experienced through shared-prayer is a powerful catalyst for building a spirit of Christian community!

Turning off the main lights in the room and setting a lit candle on a table in the center of the group will help to effect a prayerful atmosphere before beginning the praying phase. The praying phase will entail approximately one-fourth of the total meeting time.

Refreshments
Refreshments are served after the end of the praying phase of the meeting, providing an opportunity for the young people to socialize and fellowship as long as they wish to stay. Initially the team leaders should arrange for refreshments (soft drinks, punch, cookies, donuts, etc.), for each meeting. Members can be asked to provide the refreshments for the meetings once the program has commenced, although leaders should always have a contingency plan ready in case it is needed.

Music
Music is a tremendous means of preparing a warm receptive environment as the young people arrive for the meeting. Christian music or suitable contemporary music can be provided by records. If some of the young people play guitars, bongo drums, flutes, etc., encourage them to bring their instruments and lead the group in several songs of praise and worship before the meetings begin, at appropriate times during the meetings, and to conclude the meetings after the completion of the shared-prayer.

Evaluations

At the final meeting of a series request written evaluations of the series from the young people. One approach is to ask them if they were to repeat this exact same series of meetings again, what did they like most and would want emphasized, and what did they like least and would want changed? Also invite suggestions for future series study themes and books of the Bible they are particularly interested in studying. Such evaluations will greatly assist the youth Scripture leaders and catechists in their future program planning.

Final Meeting of a Series

The concluding meeting of a series should be a specially planned celebration. It can include a special liturgy planned and prepared by the young people. They select the liturgy theme, the Scripture readings and music, as well as planning for lectors, participants in the offertory procession, and other special liturgical arrangements. An appropriate time during the liturgy should be provided for inviting the youth to give personal testimony, if any wish, of how Jesus Christ has "touched" their lives during this series of meetings, and through their experience of Scripture, community, prayer and service. Following the liturgy, refreshments prepared by the young people are served and a time for fellowship concludes the series.

ROLE OF LEADERS

Team leadership in the youth ministry Scripture groups has the same value and purpose as it does in the adult Scripture programs. The team of two persons may consist of an engaged couple, married couple, a priest or religious and lay person, etc. The team acts together as discussion leaders or catechists for each group of eight to twelve young people. Their mutual support and shared responsibility in the presentation of the study input, facilitation of the group sharing and praying of Scripture are not only a witness to the youth involved, but also a catalyst for maintaining order and interest within a given meeting.

Leadership Training

Youth ministry Scripture group leadership requires that the adults involved "must be trained to deal with youth and to transmit authentic values . . . living the Gospel message so that young people not only understand it but see it exemplified" (Statement on Youth Ministry, by Cardinal Timothy Manning). In addition to their diocesan youth catechist training, the discussion leaders and catechists should avail themselves of Scripture Program leadership training or participate in an ongoing home or parish Scripture program to obtain the necessary understanding and experience of the study, share and pray format for subsequent adaptation in the youth Scripture groups.

Leadership Qualities

It is essential that persons wishing to teach and lead youth Scripture groups personally have a familiarity and love of God's Word and are persons of prayer, who not only profess knowledge of their religion, but more importantly, live their faith! In an almost indescribable way, youth leaders "teach and preach" the Word of God more by their attitudes and actions than by all the things they will ever say to the youth! Their lives are "Living Words" spreading the "Good News." The love of God through the Scripture that the leaders aim to teach will be more *caught* by the youth through who the leaders are and how they act, than *taught* by what they say and teach!

A special love and understanding of young people should characterize the youth leader's every attitude and approach from the initial program planning through to the meeting leadership.

Leadership Responsibilities

The youth ministry team is responsible for arranging a suitable and comfortable meeting place (leader's home, church lounge, etc.), simple refreshments and for appropriate audio-visual equipment and other resource materials required for the meetings.

Initially the leader team should preview materials and develop the overall plan for the youth ministry Scripture Program. As the young people's personal interest in study, sharing and praying of Scripture matures, they may want to have greater involvement in the planning and even in the presentation of the study and prayer phases of the meetings. When this occurs the youth ministry Scripture leader team will preview material and select several suggested themes and approaches for the **STUDY phase**. Fortified with this background information and a selection of resource materials, the leader team can offer several alternative themes and study approaches to the youth, letting the group determine the specific theme and study approaches for a given series.

Peer-Leadership Development

The aim of youth ministry leadership in Scripture Programs is for the youth themselves to assume growing responsibility for shared leadership under the recognized leader-team. The more interested youth should be led to form a "core" group that can work together with the leader-team in future program planning and presentations. The more fully the "core" group can be involved in the selection of Scripture themes and the preparation of the study and the praying phases, the more committed they will become! The entire group's motivation for community service, Christian action and peer evangelization will be a measure of how the vitality of God's Word finds application and meaning in their lives! As the youth ministry Scripture program membership increases, the more experienced and committed young adults should be encouraged to move into roles of group leadership for the new and younger members.

Community-Building

Community-Building is of special concern and demands regular attention by youth ministry Scripture leaders. Every meeting should include within its meeting schedule a period of time for fellowship and social sharing. Group faith-building by sharing faith-experiences, personal witnessing and peer evangelization will all be the catalysts for enlivening the spirit of Christian community among the young people. Service projects stemming from Scripture study and sharing should also aim to involve as many of the youth at a given time as possible. An allotted time during each meeting for individual reporting on personal acts of Christian service or evangelization resulting from actions chosen at a previous meeting will also work toward building a sense of community.

A closing liturgy, planned and participated in by the youth at the end of each series, often confirms the growth of community they have experienced through their study, sharing, praying—and, most importantly, living Scripture together.

Personal invitations by the team leaders and some of the highly involved youth encouraging their friends to return to future series will always be the greatest publicity for program growth in membership.

ALTERNATE STUDY TECHNIQUES FOR YOUTH INVOLVEMENT

Following are a number of study-input techniques that are usually quite effective with young people, especially those who feel they have to be in the class, rather than having freely chosen to attend. Each of these study techniques involve the youth to some degree and are aimed at gradually preparing and encouraging them to enter more seriously into studying, sharing and praying the Word of God. To be most effective each study technique should usually be used only once during a series or a program year.

These study techniques were used when we were team-teaching in our parish high-school C.C.D. and later in our youth home Scripture groups. All of the approaches were well received and enjoyed by the youth in those groups. In some cases the group sharing became a logical extention of the **STUDY phase**, or evolved easily out of certain techniques at the conclusion of what had been learned through the study input. Group shared prayer or praying of Scripture concluded a typical meeting.

The goal to be kept in mind when choosing a study technique is that everything that is taught is meant to be more than just head knowledge. The catechist's aim, through involving the youth as much as possible in every aspect of a meeting, should be to make what is being taught personal heart knowledge, to be understood and experienced in light of the Gospel message and through the experience of community sharing. The occasional use of some of these study techniques in more mature youth Scripture groups will most always be rewarding and a welcome change-of-pace for a meeting.

1. Serendipity

Lyman Coleman's *Encyclopedia of Serendipity* is an invaluable tool for youth leaders, especially for use in youth Scripture groups. There are dozens of crowd-breaker techniques, communication exercises and group building sessions that can be used to help the young people to get involved and acquainted with one another. Every youth meeting could beneficially use one or more of these "games" or exercises to help create a relaxed, informal and open atmosphere at the beginning of a meeting or at mid-meeting for a change-of-pace. Most of the crowd-breaker techniques and communication exercises take less than five minutes. Those five minutes can sometimes set or change the tone or direction of an entire meeting!

Within the *Encyclopedia of Serendipity* there are eight Bible study creative techniques. These techniques, as well as the 36 structured Scripture sessions, offer a wide selection of very effective study techniques that are usually well received by any age group of young people. Refer to chapter 4, Parish Scripture Programs, alternative #4, and to alternative #2 in this chapter, for detailed meeting and series examples using Serendipity methods.

2. Question with Anonymous Answers

An effective technique for involving all the participants in sharing their personal thoughts and feelings about a certain subject is to pose a question and ask all the youth to each anonymously write out his/her answer on a sheet of paper. The pieces of paper are collected, shuffled and then redistributed to the members, being sure no one receives his/her own answer. In sequence, each member reads the answer on his/her paper, following it with a personal positive comment upon what was read. After everyone has read an answer and offered comments, the leaders direct the discussion into a general sharing of what has been learned through this study input and what it means to them.

The kind of questions asked support the chosen study theme while allowing for personal reflection and expression by each member in his/her answer. Questions such as: Who is Jesus Christ to/for you? . . . What does Faith mean to you? . . . How do you live your Faith? . . . What does Prayer mean for you? . . . How do you usually pray (ways, circumstances, etc.)? . . . What do the Sacraments mean to you? . . . What does the Mass mean to you? . . . What does Christian Community mean to/for you? . . . What does the Bible mean to/for you? . . .

What does (a certain passage of Scripture) mean to you personally?...

3. Homemade Slides

After a brief teaching and group discussion on the study theme, the youth are asked to select pictures from magazines that are suitable to make into slides that portray their personal understanding of the study theme. Directions for making homemade slides and a list of the required materials are available in many catechetical methodology manuals. During the activity of making the slides, record music is played and community sharing is also taking place. The prayer time consists of showing the slides the youth have made. With a degree of anonymity in the darkened room, the young people are asked to speak out when their slide(s) are shown, telling what the scene is, why they chose it, and how they "see" God present in it. The slide-prayer session concludes with shared group prayer. Some suitable study themes for making slides are: God's Presence in the World Today, The Be-Attitudes, Living (each of the) Sacraments, Christian Living, Signs of the "Living-Word," The Living-Out of the Liturgy, and The "Sheep" of Matthew 25:31–46.

One of the most moving prayer-experiences with youth occurred during such a slide prayer session. The study theme was "The Eucharist" and the slides were "seeing God's presence around us." About three-fourths of the way through the slides an all black slide came up. Taken momentarily by surprise and thinking it was a mistake, we were moving on to the next slide when a boy's voice quietly caught our attention. "That's mine. I made it black. I can't find God anyplace. I don't know Him." The impact on everyone was indescribable! Later as the "touched" young people shared their prayers, the presence of God could truly be "felt"! It was an experience of peer-evangelization, youth-to-youth ministry, that affected all of us.

4. Homilies

This study technique involves some individual preparation by the young people prior to the meeting. The leaders select a number of Scripture passages (5 to 20 verses in length) that develop a theme, i.e., discipleship, love, forgiveness, service, a variety of parables, or examples of different miracles. *Nave's Topical Index* by Orville Nave is a useful resource for selecting Scripture passages that develop a study theme. The young people choose one of the suggested passages from which they prepare a 2 to 5 minute "homily." In their homilies, they are asked to (1) explain something of the background THEN-context of the passage; and (2) the NOW-context of the meaning of the passage in their daily lives.

During the following meeting, each young person presents his or her homily. After all the homilies are presented, giving different facets of the study theme, the leaders guide the youth into group sharing concerning what they have learned and the personal application

found for their lives. One of the passages is then used for the **PRAYING SCRIPTURE phase** to conclude the meeting.

5. Parable Charades

The preparation that is required for this study technique is also very conducive to community-building among the youth. Preparation can be either between the meetings or done during the first part of a meeting. Parable charades is "played" in the same way as the parlor game of charades. Groups of three to four young people are given a pre-selected parable compatible with the theme of the meeting and requested to act out its story in a charade. All the youth should be involved. A member of each group reads the parable for their group, they discuss its meaning and how they will act it out. Props or songs can be used, although there is no talking permitted during the acting-out of the charade. Each group performs their "parable" and the other members must guess which one it is and find it in Scripture (if they are familiar enough with Scripture to do so). After the charades, the leaders guide the youth into a group discussion of the meaning of the parables, why Jesus used them, what is the meaning of their charade parables, and how do they see the same parables applicable to their present lives. One of the parables is read again, shared and prayed during the **PRAYING phase** of the meeting.

Some of the many parables that are excellent for charades include: Parable of the Seed—Matthew 13:4–23; The Weeds—Matthew 13:24–29; The Straying Sheep—Matthew 18:10–14; Laborers in the Vineyard—Matthew 20:1–16; Parable of the Two Sons—Matthew 21:28–32; The Wedding Banquet—Matthew 22:1–14; Parable of the Ten Virgins—Matthew 25:1–13; Parable of the Silver Pieces—Matthew 25:14–30; The Last Judgment—Matthew 25:31–46; The Good Samaritan—Luke 10:25–27; Preparedness for the Master's Return—Luke 12:35–48; The Banquet—Luke 14:12–24; The Prodigal Son—Luke 15:11–15; The Rich Man and Lazarus—Luke 17:19–31; The Corrupt Judge—Luke 18:1–18; and The Parable of the Sum of Money—Luke 19:11–27.

6. Contemporary Parables

This study technique should appropriately follow after the parable-charades or other teachings on the parables. To begin the meeting, the leaders lead the youth into a group discussion on the purpose of the parables, THEN and NOW. Discuss how they think Christ might express certain parables today to teach the same lessons or to convey a similar message. What kinds of symbols and analogies would be better understood and more applicable for the people today?

After the initial discussion, a parable is selected and the young people are asked to contemporize it, using symbols, analogies or situations that are applicable to the language and understanding of 20th-century people, while still retaining its basic lesson or message. The re-write can be done as an individual activity either during or outside of the time of the meeting. Or a more effective community-building approach is to divide the youth at the meeting into small groups of three to four members who mutually work together and jointly re-write the parable. Allow half an hour for the groups to re-write their parables before asking each group to read their contemporary parable. Select parables to be contemporized from the list of parables given in the previous study technique (#5).

A group discussion about what the study involvement has meant and taught them concludes the **STUDY** and **SHARING phases**. One of the Scripture parables should be chosen for **PRAYING of Scripture** to end the meeting.

7. Bible Drama
Youth group members often enjoy the challenge experienced in the preparation and presentation of a Bible drama. The events, lives of the people and words of Scripture take on deeper meaning through the youth's involvement in such dramatic re-enactments. *Bible As Drama* by Rev. Lawrence Waddy is an outstanding resource book containing 90 Bible stories presented as plays. Included are both Old and New Testament stories of varying lengths.

Youth leaders and the participating youth should together select and plan the preparation and the presentation of the Bible dramas. After a presentation, group discussion about the importance and meaning of the related Scripture passages will make this study technique an effective learning experience. The same passage, or part of the passage, should also be used during the **PRAYING SCRIPTURE phase** of the meeting.

8. Biblical Role Playing
Taking less preparation than a structured Bible drama, the biblical role playing can be improvised on a moment's notice. In the middle of a program teaching or a group sharing, the leaders can suggest role playing of the Scripture event being studied or discussed. Improvised dialogue on the events of Christ's life, Old Testament events, the miracle stories and parables, or the attitudes and responses of persons in relationship with Jesus Christ can be an enriching way of learning the message of the Scriptures. Through group discussion and role playing the youth are led to understand the meaning of the biblical events, the attitudes, responses and feelings of the persons in each event, and they are encouraged to imagine how they would act today in similar instances.

9. Special Guests
Inviting special guests to share in a youth Scripture group is another study approach. The selection of the guests and reasons for their coming might be considered the study technique. The young people's awareness of how people respond to their "call" to live-out their Christian commitment in light of the understanding of the Gospel message is an important aspect of studying and sharing Scripture. By their personal testimonies and the examples of their lives these people reflect the Living Word of God among us. These points should be kept in mind when selecting potential guest speakers. A "key" question to pose to them in suggesting the theme of their presentation might be: "What difference does your personal relationship with Jesus Christ make in how you understand and live-out your 'call' as a . . .?"

Consider inviting several (2 to 4) guests for a single meeting, who because of their ages and experiences are at different stages of understanding and living-out their "call." For example: a young seminarian, a deacon and/or a priest ordained over 25 years; a novice sister and a religious professed over 25 years; an engaged couple and a couple married over 25 years, or even over 50 years; etc. An informal question and answer time, followed by a group sharing and discussions involving the guests, is invaluable.

10. The Gospel According To . . .
Near the end of a series or a program year, the young people are asked to write their own "gospel"! Through his/her "gospel" each person can share the good news of the personal Jesus Christ they have grown to know, love and experience within their lives through Scripture and in their community. This special project is only possible after the group has been meeting for a long enough time so that the members feel free and comfortable for such personal sharing. All members should be gently encouraged to try to write their own "gospel." In the event some may not choose to do so—that is all right. A couple of weeks should be allowed for this project to be performed outside of the meeting time. At a predetermined meeting the youth can each read their "gospel according to . . . (their name)" for the group. As these "gospels" are shared, leaders should encourage the youth to look and listen for the Christ revealed in each "gospel" through these contemporary evangelists writing for their community of believers! The youth leaders should consider the possibility of compiling all the "gospels" into a mimeographed booklet for each participant to keep as a reminder of his/her community experience of meeting Christ together.

11. The Epistle To . . .
The youth leaders ask the young people to each think of a group of people, a community of believers, to whom they would like to write a letter—an "epistle." It should be a group or community to which the young person personally belongs and has personal interest and concern for its members. The group or community could be a young person's immediate family, a group of closest friends, the youth Scripture group itself, their parish community, or even their country. The youth leader's teachings on the life of St. Paul and his letters written for his communities will provide the scriptural example of the kind of "epistle" the young people are being asked

to write. In their "epistles" the youth can share: their expectations for the community; the gifts they see in the members; cautions they would want to bring to the members' attention; their faith, hope and love for the community; the "call" of Jesus they see for the community; their need for the community's support and prayers; and their personal prayer for the members of the community.

At a subsequent meeting time, arrange for the participants to read the "epistles" that are written to the community of the youth Scripture group, as if they were received as personal letters to be shared within the community! Those youth who wrote their "epistles" to groups other than the youth Scripture community can also be invited to share them with the entire group, if they wish. Sometimes the "epistles" may be to the family and the writer may wish to keep it personal. The leaders should encourage the young writers to give their "epistles" to the intended addressees or communities. For those who would want their "epistles" included, the leaders should consider the possibility of also compiling the "espistles" into a mimeographed booklet, along with the "gospels," for each member of the youth Scripture group.

FIRST-YEAR THEME DEVELOPMENT AND TYPICAL MEETINGS

When the youth Scripture Programs are presented in "blocks" during the school year, such as three series each six to eight meetings in length, there is some latitude for selecting the biblical themes for each series. Often the turnover of young people from one series to another will limit extended development of a theme except by overlapping several series. The choice of the theme and the extent of its development will depend therefore upon how long the leaders expect the same group of young people to be in a specific program. If they will be together for the full school year, much more can be presented and accomplished!

As important as it is for the young people to have an opportunity to gain an overview of the great themes of the Old and New Testaments, this theme may need to be considered primarily for the more mature and committed youth in ongoing programs. It may also depend upon the resource material chosen by the youth program catechists. For example, *Discovering the Bible* by Rev. John Tickle provides study, sharing and prayer guides covering eight themes in the Old and New Testament, which can be used for either eight meetings (combining the Old and New Testament study of each theme) or else extended to two series covering sixteen meetings.

Two outstanding youth Scripture study guides and commentaries that are most effectively used for an extended program (full school year or three successive series) are *These Stones Will Shout—A New Voice for the Old Testament* and *The Seventh Trumpet—The Good News Proclaimed* both by Mark Link, S.J., *Man Meets God—The Great Themes of Scripture* by Rev. Robert Humitz and *Understanding the Bible* by Thomas Zimmerman and Ronald Wilkins, are each study guides that may be used either by selected chapters for a series or in their entirety for a full year program. These resources each have a teacher's manual available.

If there is only a single series of six to eight meetings with a select group of young people, then the priority on choice of themes should appropriately be directed toward introducing them personally to Jesus Christ as he is revealed in one of the Synoptic Gospels. There are some excellent study resources available to guide catechists in choosing the series theme and providing background content for their teachings. Sections or chapters from the study guides can be selected for use in the teachings when a series length does not allow for the use of the entire book. In addition to using a study guide to develop the theme of the series and to prepare their teaching, catechists should try to incorporate additional study approaches, i.e., short sections of taped talks, audiovisuals and guest speakers, as well as some special study techniques for program variety.

Following are Scripture study guides that provide solid content and theme development suitable for either a series or an extended full year program. Each book has an accompanying teacher's manual that suggests study techniques and methods for involving the youth.

A Journey to Emmaus by Jeanne Heiberg

Real Living from the Encounter Series

Caring: Heart of the Gospel from The Center for Learning Series

Scripture: Good News About You from The Center for Learning Series

The JESUS Book from the To Live As Christ Series

In Search of Jesus from The Center for Learning Series

Following are three examples of youth series that list themes, resources and suggested alternative study approaches and techniques for meeting variety. The description of a typical meeting or meeting outlines for each series is based on the primary study input being provided by the catechist's teachings. In each example, the study, sharing and praying format is *adapted* to the circumstances and needs of each group.

Example No. 1
*Theme: **Meeting Christ in Matthew's Gospel***

Series length: six 1½ hour meetings.

Resources: regular speaker (catechist), books and tapes used by catechist for his/her teaching preparation.

Books:
Man Meets God, R. Humitz

Gospel of St. Matthew, D. Senior

Invitation to Matthew, D. Senior

Seventh Trumpet, M. Link

The Gospel of Matthew, Volumes 1 and 2, W. Barclay

Tapes:
Matthew's Good News—The Reign of God (Jesus and His Church series), R. Rohr

The Gospels of Matthew and Luke (Toward Understanding the New Testament series), E. LaVerdiere

Gospel of Matthew (Enjoying the New Testament series), G. Montague

The Gospel of Matthew (4 cassettes), Joseph Grassi

Meeting Study Input Outline:

Meeting #1 *Explanation of youth Scripture Program format and Get Acquainted Time.*
Teaching, *He Is Present in His Word*
(Background on Bible formation and the Gospel of Matthew)
Scripture prayer passage: *Proverbs 4:20–22*

Meeting #2 Teaching, *Preaching of the Good News of the Kingdom of God*
(Matthew 1 through 7, special emphasis on the Beatitudes)
Scripture prayer passage: *Matthew 5:14–16*

Meeting #3 Teaching, *A Call to be a Disciple: A Disciple of Whom?*
(Matthew 8 through 13, Jesus' ministry and call of his disciples)
Scripture prayer passage: *Matthew 8:23–27*

Meeting #4 Teaching, *We Experience the Kingdom as Church*
(Matthew 13:54; 20:34, Jesus' healings, miracles, deliverance, feeding the 4,000 and calling Peter the "Rock")
prayer passage: *Matthew 20:27–29*

Meeting #5 Teaching, *The Kingdom as Church*
(Matthew 21 through 28, Jesus' ministry culminates with the mystery of the Eucharist, the Paschal Mystery and Jesus' command to "go spread the good news")
Scripture prayer passage: *Matthew 28:18–20*

Meeting #6 *Celebration of Eucharist*, followed by *Dessert and Social*

A Typical Meeting (#5) of Example No. 3

Following is the fifth meeting of this series as described by one of the team leaders of a group of eleven young people, ages 16 to 19 years. This series was presented as a summer program for interested young people and held in the catechist's home, although conducted under the parish youth ministry program structure.

A record by Keith Green entitled *For Him Who Has Ears To Hear* was played low in the background during the first fifteen minutes of sharing. The meeting was begun with a prayer.

STUDY phase:
The youth were asked to open their Bibles to Acts 2:22–24, 32–33, which was the first preached sermon of the early Church. The leaders, teaching as a team, each shared in the presentation, adding information to emphasize certain points made by the other. Some of the subjects touched upon were Jesus' ministry from chapter 20 through chapter 25, with emphasis on the teachings that symbolized the Church as the Kingdom on earth. Also highlighted were the gifts of the Father, the gift of the Eucharist given to us in the midst of betrayal, and our Lord's final gift in Matthew 28:18, the establishment of the Church and his promise to be with us always. During the teaching there were questions from the youth and intermittent discussions.

SHARING phase:
The leaders planned to conduct a para-liturgical ceremony, an agape, during the **SHARING phase**. They started by placing twelve different kinds of glasses on the coffee table. Some of them were coke glasses, beer mugs, a glass with a Bugs Bunny decal, a copper mug, a jelly glass, a plastic water glass and a crystal goblet. The young people were asked to look them over and pick the one that would most represent how they thought they would feel at the Last Supper with Jesus. They were to make this judgment by how they responded to either the shape or color of the glass. The leaders then poured a small amount of grape juice in each person's container. A small loaf of uncut French bread was passed around and each person broke off a piece. As all silently ate the bread and drank the juice, they were asked to meditate on the Last Supper. The song *I Don't Know*

How To Love Him from the album, "Jesus Christ Superstar," was played during the agape. Afterward each member shared why he/she picked that particular glass.

PRAYING SCRIPTURE phase:
Matthew 28:18–20
Insight was "Jesus Is Alive!"

The parish gave them permission to use the Paschal Candle from the altar as their prayer-candle. After a brief explanation of the meaning of the Paschal Candle, it was set in the center of the group, lit by a member (other lights turned off) and the Scripture was read by the light of the candle.

First reading—followed by silent reflection and meditation on what this promise of Jesus meant to the apostles and how it must have made them feel.

Second reading—followed again by silent reflection and then group sharing of what Jesus' promise means personally in the life of each of the young people present.

Third reading—followed by silent reflection and then group shared praying of the Scripture passage. The group prayer was concluded by lifting their individual needs and thanks to the Lord.

Lights were turned on, home Scripture readings were suggested for the next meeting and refreshments were served.

Conclusion by the Team-leaders:

"These meetings have proved to us that young people are hungry for Scripture. They were all interested in continuing the program into a Fall series. Everyone had a different book they wanted to study. Their main comment was that they wanted to progress slower and not try to cover so much in a single meeting. Several young people said that they had been searching for this kind of Catholic Scripture study and community sharing and prayer with other youth for a long time."

Example No. 2
Theme: **Meeting Christ in Mark's Gospel**

Series' length: eight 1½ hour meetings, but could be extended to a full year program.

Resources: regular speaker (catechist), books, filmstrip with record, and use of 2 or 3 alternative study techniques.

Books:
The Mustard Seed, by M. Link, S.J.

Encyclopedia of Serendipity, by L. Coleman

Audio-Visual
Mark—Christian Kerygma, by T. Keegan

Alternative Study Techniques:
Study Technique #7—Biblical Role Playing.

Study Techniques #1—Serendipity Bible Study Technique & Scripture Sessions:

(a) *Peter's Emotional Pilgrimage*, Mark 1:16–18,

(b) *Time Out for Checking Strategy*, Mark 4:3–8 (Parable of the Sower),

(c) *Feeling the Pressure*, Mark 4:30–32 (Parable of the Mustard Seed),

(d) *To the Rescue*, Mark 2:1–12 (Roof removed to get paralytic to Jesus),

(e) *Bucking the Pressure*, Mark 4:35–41 (Jesus calms the storm).

A Typical Meeting of Example No. 1, with Teaching Given by Youth Catechist

The meeting opens with singing led by a young person providing musical accompaniment, which is followed by the youth leader praying for God's blessings upon the group and their purpose in meeting together. A twenty minute teaching on the selected study theme and related Scripture passages is given by the catechist. General group discussion follows, facilitated by the youth leaders, on the content of the teaching and its message for the lives of the young people. Before concluding the first **SHARING phase**, a few minutes are allotted for reports on past service projects, and discussions about future service actions which will be accomplished by the group or individual members. The general group sharing lasts about twenty minutes before the youth are asked to divide into small groups of 3 to 4 members. Each young person has his/her own copy of *The Mustard Seed* or a mimeographed copy of the Scripture passages related to the teaching. In silence for about five minutes, the young people are asked to write out their personal reflections relative to the teaching and the Scripture passage(s). Then within their small groups, the members are asked to share with one another what they wrote and their reasons why! The aim in this second **SHARING phase** is for personal reflection and sharing that leads to peer feedback and support—literally the experience of youth ministering to youth! This phase lasts about fifteen minutes. The leaders then lead the groups in Scripture prayer, using the same (or one of the) passages already studied and shared earlier in the meeting. The shared praying of Scripture is done within the small groups. When Scripture praying is concluded, the entire group of young people are invited to join together, holding hands if desired, and pray for the expressed needs and intentions of one another, before closing the one and a half hour meeting with a song. Time for refreshments and fellowship should always be made available after the conclusion of the meeting.

Example No. 3
Theme: *Meeting Christ in Luke's Gospel*

Series' length: ongoing weekly one hour meetings preceding the parish prayer meeting.

Resources: regular speaker (catechist) and books.

Books:
The New American Bible

Gospel of St. Luke, by R. Karris

Invitation to Luke, by R. Karris

The description of this typical meeting is representative of a community of young people who have chosen to meet together regularly because of their personal encounter with Jesus Christ. They have an expressed desire to enter more seriously into his Word through the study, sharing and praying of Scripture. The study of Scripture is done chapter by chapter or passage by passage (of 5 to 25 verses) at each meeting until the entire Gospel is covered. Since their meeting time is limited to an hour, the **PRAYING SCRIPTURE phase** is adapted to a study, share and pray format as described in the meeting outline below:

Study
Teaching: 10 minutes
Introduction of the Scripture passage, focusing on the background study of the times, people and the message.

First Reading of Passage, followed by

Group Sharing: 15 minutes
directed toward a personal understanding of the THEN-context, its meaning for the people who first heard it, how they must have felt about it, responded to it, etc., the person of Jesus revealed in the passage, etc.

Teaching: 10 minutes
focusing on the meaning of the Scripture passage for man today, in society, in the Church and personally.

Sharing
Second Reading, followed by quiet reflection and *Group Sharing:* 15 minutes
directed toward personal understanding of the meaning and application of the passage in the NOW-context of contemporary life.

Praying
Third Reading, followed by quiet reflection and then *Group Praying:* 10 minutes
in which the personal sharings are formed as prayers of praise, petition, contrition, adoration or thanksgiving based on the three previous readings, and group sharings concerning the Scripture passage.

Using this suggested format, as outlined above, the following series of commentaries and prayer guides are exceptional resources for catechists' teaching preparation, as well as adaptable for use directly with the high-school seniors and college youth who want to more seriously study and pray Scripture.

Gospel of St. Matthew, from the Read and Pray series, D. Senior

Invitation to Matthew, A Commentary, D. Senior

Gospel of St. Mark, from the Read and Pray series, P. Van Linden

Invitation to Mark, A Commentary, P. Achtemeier

Gospel of St. John, from the Read and Pray series, P. Perkins

Invitation to John, A Commentary, G. MacRae.

The following four sets of taped talks are most complementary to the above listed books, providing commentary, along with contemporary spiritual insights for each of the Gospels.

The Gospel of Matthew, The Gospel of Mark, The Gospel of Luke, and *The Gospel of John*, four sets by Joseph Grassi.

ALTERNATIVE STUDY APPROACHES AND STRUCTURES

As mentioned before, the initial goal should be a year-long program, or successive series, developing the overview of the Old and New Testament. When restricted to a singular series, the first series of a youth Scripture Program should be directed toward introducing the youth to Jesus Christ as He is revealed in the Synoptic Gospels and as He can be experienced through community sharing and prayer. Succeeding series themes and study approaches can be as variable as the ingenuity of the youth catechists and the expressed interests of the young people in each group!

All of the previously listed books in this chapter are recommended for subsequent series with the aim of continuing to deepen the youth's knowledge and understanding of Scripture. An outstanding Scripture Commentary with accompanying catechist's study manual is available as a set of books on the Acts of the Apostles, entitled *Alive In The Spirit* by Thomas Smith. In light of the faith development of the Christian community in the early Church revealed in the Acts, the catechist can easily draw parallels for the youth in understanding their own faith development within the contemporary Christian community of the Church.

Another important facet of helping youth deepen their encounter with Jesus Christ, is to provide a series that will enable them to recognize his presence in their reception of the Sacraments. An exceptional set of books (a youth's manual and a teacher's manual) that will assist the youth catechist in this goal is entitled *A Journey To Emmaus: Recognizing the Lord* by Jeanne Heiberg. This set of books combines solid teaching guidelines for study input by the catechist, various study techniques involving the youth, group sharing, and Scripture passages that can be used for group prayer.

Different family and parish situations often give birth to multiple ways of helping the youth to study, share and pray God's Word together. Following are descriptions of some of the alternative study approaches and program structures for youth Scripture groups that have either been personally experienced or shared with us by youth leaders in the Los Angeles Archdiocese. Again, a reminder, two of the key descriptive words for any youth leader, catechist or program are "flexibility" and "adaptability"!

Alternative No. 1

In the introduction to this chapter reference was made to a youth Scripture group involving seven teenagers and their four parents. During the summer of 1974, as parents we came to the acute awareness that there was both need and desire to re-evaluate our responsibilities as parent-educators and to examine how we could share more personally the Christ we had grown to know and love with our young people. Another couple shared similar concern with us and together we realized we cannot give "our faith" to our children. Recognizing that faith is a gift, our goal was to enable our young people to be prepared to more fully receive and exercise their gift of faith as they matured. We hoped to encourage our teenagers to develop a sense of openness and expectancy in living their faith through an understanding of the message of God's love in Scripture and in the experience of community sharing and praying within the two families.

Since none of us as parents felt adequately qualified to "teach" Scripture, we depended upon the taped talks on the *Great Themes of Scripture* by Rev. Richard Rohr, O.F.M., along with the study guide, *Man Meets God* by Rev. Robert Humitz. With these two resources as background information we prepared weekly study presentations. As couples, we alternately presented about a twenty minute study input. We found out it was more successful with the age of our teenagers to develop a presentation from the resource material and present it as a parent-educator couple. Many of the study techniques described earlier were frequently included in these meetings. Since neither of the families had previously read the books of the Old Testament, each family arranged time between the meetings for nightly quarter-hour periods of family shared Scripture reading. In addition to the Scripture readings, we found the Reader's Digest *Great People of the Bible and How They Lived* to be an exceptional enrichment book enjoyed by everyone. Initially to aid all of us in entering into group shared-prayer at each meeting, we depended upon the numerous "how-to" guides in *Experiments In Prayer* by Betsy Caprio. As we became more comfortable as a group with shared prayer, we began to turn to Scripture prayer more frequently to end our meetings. Special activities were planned periodically during the year, including filmstrips and a film, a guest speaker, an experience of participating in a home Paschal Meal, and two home Liturgies which the youth helped prepare.

Following is a general outline of the meeting themes and study resources we used in preparation for the teachings as well as the special activities we shared with the youth. Also included are the suggested home Scripture readings we shared as a family between the meetings.

This alternative meeting series could easily be adapted to a parish setting for a year-long or multi-series youth Scripture Program overview of the Old and New Testament.

Suggested Meeting Outline

Meeting	Resources Used for Preparing Teachings or Special Activities for a Meeting	Home Reading
#1	Tape #1, *The Call: Introduction to the Word*	
#2	Man Meets God, pp. 7–14	Exodus
#3	Tape #2, *Exodus: The Journey of Faith*	
#4	Man Meets God, pp. 15–30	Joshua to Kings (excerpts)
#5	Tape #3, *Joshua to Kings: Ordinary Becomes Extraordinary*	
#6	Man Meets God, pp. 31–44	Prophet Isaiah (1, 6, 9, 11, 40–66)
#7	Special Activity: *Guest Speaker*	

Meeting	Resources Used for Preparing Teachings or Special Activities for a Meeting	Home Reading
#8	Tape #4, *Prophets: Radical Traditionalists*	
#9	*Man Meets God* pp. 45–62	Genesis
#10	Tape #5, *Genesis: God and Man* (first half of tape)	
#11	*Man Meets God*, pp. 63–68	Job (excerpts)
#12	Tape #5, *Job: Good and Evil* (last half of tape)	
#13	Special Activity: *Home Liturgy* (Christmas)	Selected Psalms
#14	Tape #6, *Salvation History: Faith in Evolution*	
#15	*Man Meets God* pp. 69–74	Gospel of Matthew (Read entirely at one sitting)
#16	Tape #7, *Gospel of Matthew: The Reign of God*	Matthew 26–28
#17	*Man Meets God* pp. 75–88	Matthew 3–11
#18	*Man Meets God* pp. 89–103	Matthew 8–13
#19	*Man Meets God* pp. 104–108	Matthew 13:54–25:46
#20	*Man Meets God* pp. 109–120	
#21	Special Activity: Two Filmstrips—(Alpha-Omega Co.) *Exodus of Israel* and *Exodus of Jesus*	Gospel of Mark (excerpts)
#22	Tape #8, *Mark: Jesus Is Lord* (first half of talk)	
#23	Tape #8, *John, Jesus Is Lord* (last half of talk)	
#24	Tape #9, *Luke and Acts: A New Life*	Acts of the Apostles
#25	*Man Meets God*, pp. 121–129	
#26	Special Activity: *Paschal Meal* following Holy Thursday Mass at Church.	Paul's Epistles (sections of different Epistles assigned to each youth, for each to report back on in subsequent meetings)

Meeting	Resources Used for Preparing Teachings or Special Activities for a Meeting	Home Reading
#27	Tape #11, *Paul: A Life in Christ*	
#28	*Man Meets God*, pp. 130–136	
#29	Tape #10, *Mary, Prayer and Church*	
#30	Special Activity: Film—*Charismatic Renewal in the Church*	
#31	Special Activity: Group Attend a Youth Prayer Meeting in Area	
#32	Tape #12, *Apocalypse: The New Creation*	
#33	*Man Meets God*, pp. 147–154	
#34	Special Activity: *Home Liturgy* planned by youth to conclude the program year	

Alternative No. 2

Parents often express their desire to be more involved with their older children (teenagers and young adults especially) in sharing their faith-experiences and beliefs. If they are not trained as youth catechists they may feel inadequate, questioning where and how they could meet this challenge within their families. Lyman Coleman has developed a variety of Serendipity program books that are ideal aids for both parents and catechists working with young people. Each book develops a theme through sixteen sharing techniques and Scripture sessions. The *Encyclopedia of Serendipity* contains 36 of these Scripture sessions which have been extracted from a set of three books described by Lyman Coleman as "our answer to the young scene today for a study series on the basics of the Christian life." The books are available separately so that each member participating in the family-sharing has his/her own set of questionnaires. The titles and themes of these three books are:

Breaker 1-9—for getting your life together;

10-4, Good Buddy—for building relationships; and

Movin' On—for developing moral character.

Another set of books not included in the *Encyclopedia of Serendipity* Scripture sessions are the personal growth programs. These are each especially geared toward family sharing, although many of the sessions can also be adapted for either youth Scripture groups or adult Scripture Programs. The books are also available separately so each member has his/her own copy. The titles and themes of these three books are:

Come Fly—a basic which deals with the Christian lifestyle;

Hassle—which deals with family relationships;

Destiny—for discovering your own uniqueness and call in life.

After selecting one of these books, the parents plan regular or periodic sessions when all of the family members can arrange to be together for a family sharing time. An hour time limit in the beginning is advisable. After opening with a prayer, a member reads the Scripture passage to the family (group) before each person fills out the questionnaire. One by one the members share their answer to the first question until everyone has participated. Each successive question is similarly answered until all the questions are covered by the participants. Group faith-sharing and discussions will usually spontaneously flow out of the answers given by the members. The sharing often becomes so involved and enjoyable that it is necessary to remind everyone to move on to the final questions. The sharing concludes with group prayer, either by re-reading the Scripture passage with joined hands praying Scripture together, or by some other appropriate expression of prayer for one another within the family circle.

Over the period of time it takes to complete the sixteen sessions in a book, a family or youth group will inevitably experience personal and community growth in their understanding of Scripture.

When we used the *Hassle* book for our family Scripture sharings, we arranged to set aside an hour after dinner one Sunday afternoon a month. The time and frequency were chosen because it was meant simply to be a family fun time of sharing and not part of a structured religious program. The grandparents had expressed interest in our family time activity, so they also were invited to join us. The joy and enrichment of three generations of faith-sharing and mutual understanding experienced within the family was quite a gift for the youth, as well as for the parents and grandparents!

Alternative No. 3
In every parish there will likely be found a small number of young adults (usually 16 to 20 years of age) who may prefer to participate in the parish (adult) Scripture Program as part of a youth ministry table group. These are youth who are capable and willing to adapt themselves to the parish program format of study, sharing and praying Scripture. They find little difficulty maintaining interest when the study input is primarily taped talks or an hour-long teaching by speakers. Often they are young people who are already committed to a personal relationship with Jesus Christ and are sincerely interested in studying Scripture, and experiencing community and shared prayer.

With this awareness in mind, the parish Scripture Program leaders should search out and invite two young adults who are capable of assuming responsibility as youth ministry team leaders; and who are willing to lead their own table group of young people within the structure of the adult program. The only adaptations made for the young people within the program are those decided upon by the youth ministry table leaders and the young members themselves. Such adaptations will usually consist of specially composed questions geared to their level of interest (some of the adult-level questions will usually apply); and dividing up the home reading so each member does part of the overall reading so that together they cover it all. The manner of drawing forth the group sharings, the dependency upon the home reading, and the selection of special questions will all be developed by the youth ministry leaders based on the response of their table members. Youth leaders should avail themselves of the opportunity, if possible, to listen to upcoming taped talks beforehand at home, so they can gauge their questions, etc., in preparation for the meeting with the youth. Refer to the chapter on parish Scripture Programs for further details of the parish program format and resources, etc.

Alternative No. 4
The publicity techniques described earlier in this chapter are always an important "tool" for informing and interesting young people in youth Scripture Programs. An alternative approach to attracting the youth to opportunities for Christian fellowship and motivating them to learn more about Jesus Christ is through the presentation of Catholic evangelical concerts. The goal of music evangelism is "to evoke a response from the audience whereby they make explicit their acceptance of Jesus as their Lord, their commitment to follow him, and their pledge to help in the renewal of the Church." Such concerts, presented with an air of professionalism on a regular basis, usually draw forth an enthusiastic response from the young people.

Recognizing the tremendous drawing power of gospel-rock music for young people, the Southern California Renewal Communities in Los Angeles has established the S.C.R.C. Concert Ministries. The purpose and goal of Concert Ministries is: ". . . the development, organization and support of Catholic evangelical concerts. The concerts are given to serve the purpose of getting together the youth for the purpose of evangelization through song. Music touches the deepest resources of the heart and once the youth allow the music to bring forth God's Word, hopefully they will make a commitment to follow Him in a more complete way. Once the commitment is made, then the Youth Team (Ministry) for the area will be ready to help the youth grow in the Word by sharing this Word with the youth attending the concerts. Each area should have a prepared follow-up team (Youth Ministry), whose purpose is to make available:

a. Bible study group(s),

b. youth prayer meetings, and

c. the means to teach youth in scriptural and shared prayer."

As part of the concert format, the young people are invited to renew their Baptismal promises and to deepen their personal commitment to Jesus Christ. Following the concert there are refreshments and fellowship, at which time all the youth are invited to attend a follow-up sharing meeting. At the follow-up meeting the youth are provided information and an invitation to attend existing youth Bible study group(s), youth prayer meetings and other Christian fellowship activities available at area youth centers or at the parish, high schools or college campuses within their area.

Our interest in including this music ministry approach is that its purpose is integral to much we have shared in this section on youth Scripture Programs. The initial response of the youth to the concerts during the first year of the S.C.R.C. Concert Ministry programming emphasizes the potential impact the regular use of Catholic evangelical concerts can have upon the youth of the Catholic Church. For example, during the summer of 1978 *Parousia*, an evangelical gospel-rock group under the auspices of the S.C.R.C. Concert Ministries, gave an area concert that was attended by some 2,000 youth, eager to hear the Good News proclaimed in song!

The music ministry coordinator for the S.C.R.C. Concert Ministries has given permission for his name and address to be included herein. Anyone wishing further information and guidelines on Concert Ministries can contact John Clauder, Southern California Renewal Communities, 5730 W. Manchester Ave., P.O. Box 45594, Los Angeles, California 90045, (213) 645-1162.

APPENDIX A
RECOMMENDED BOOKS FOR YOUTH SCRIPTURE STUDY AND PRAYER

Some "Tools" For Gospel Study

Coleman, Lyman. *Encyclopedia of Serendipity.* Serendipity House, 1976.

Waddy, Lawrence. *The Bible As Drama.* Paulist Press, 1975.

Garvin, Mary. *Bible Study Can Be Exciting!* Zondervan Publishing House, 1976. (Practical methods of small group Bible study explained.)

The Bible and You (A Scriptographic booklet). Channing L. Bete Co., 1971.

Nave, Orville. *Nave's Topical Bible.* Guardian Press, 1975.

Kosicki, S.S.B., George W. *The Key to the Good News—Jesus Christ Is Lord!* Dove Publ., 1975.

White, Rev. Thomas and Desmond O'Donnell, O.M.I. *Renewal of Faith*—Adult Instruction in the Catholic Faith. Ave Maria Press, 1974. (A basic approach to Catholic Faith with Scripture references, prayer and discussion guides included.)

SCRIPTURE STUDY GUIDES GEARED TO YOUTH MINISTRY (TEACHER MANUAL ALSO AVAILABLE FOR EACH)

Heiberg, Jeanne. *Journey to Emmaus: Recognizing the Lord.* (A Curriculum of Sacramental Spirituality for High School). Paulist Press, 1978.

The Center for Learning series, geared to Youth Ministry. William H. Sadlier Inc.
Scripture: Good News About You (New Testament studies with personal application).
In Search of Jesus.
Values in the Word of God (Old Testament studies and personal application).
Caring: Heart of the Gospel. (The Beatitudes Lived Today.)
Sacrament: The Values of Jesus. (Sacraments in Light of the Gospel Message.)

To Live As Christ series, geared to Youth Ministry. William C. Brown and Co.
Understanding the Bible. (Introductory source book on the Bible.)
Reading the New Testament. (Guide for learning how to read the New Testament.)
The JESUS Book. (Personal significance of Jesus revealed in the New Testament.)

The Encounter Series, geared to Youth Ministry. Winston Press.
Real Living. (Small group life experience of the Gospel according to St. Luke.)
Out of Easter.
The Gospels. (A teacher resource book on Scripture teaching.)

Concern. Silver Burdett Publ. Co. (Current issues related to Biblical themes, geared to Youth Ministry.)

OLD AND NEW TESTAMENT COMMENTARIES AND STUDY GUIDES

Humitz, Rev. Robert. *Man Meets God—A Guide to the Great Themes of Revelation in Scripture.* Benzinger Press, 1973. (Teacher's manual available.)

Tickle, John. *Discovering the Bible—8 Simple Keys for Learning and Praying.* Liguori Publications, 1977. (Teacher's manual available.)

———, *These Stones Will Shout—A New Voice for the Old Testament.* Argus Communications, 1975. (Teacher's manual also available.)

Great People of the Bible and How They Lived. Reader's Digest Assoc., 1974.

Herald Biblical Study Guide Series. (Four Old Testament, Six New Testament booklets.) Franciscan Herald Press, 1972.

Link, Mark, S.J. *The Seventh Trumpet—The Good News Proclaimed.* Argus Communications, 1978. (Teacher's manual also available.)

Kirk, Rev. Albert and Rev. Robert Obach. *A Commentary on the Gospel of Matthew.* Paulist Press, 1978.

Senior, Rev. Donald. *Invitation to Matthew.* Image Book, 1977.

Link, Mark, S.J. *The Mustard Seed*—A Prayer Guide to Mark's Gospel. Argus Communications, 1974.

Achtemeier, Rev. Paul. *Invitation to Mark.* Image Book, 1978.

Karris, Rev. Robert. *Invitation to Luke.* Image Book, 1977.

MacRae, Rev. George. *Invitation to John.* Image Book, 1977.

Smith, Thomas J. *Alive in the Spirit*—The Church in the Acts of the Apostles. St. Mary's College Press, 1976. (Comes with teacher's manual.)

Farrell, Rev. Melvin. *Getting to Know Christ.* Bruce Publ. Co., 1965.

Beaumont, Jeanne. *Growing Up In Christ — The Glad News of God's Presence.* Liturgical Press, 1967. (Gospel message in easier words; good for elementary level.)

Madden, Rev. Richard. *Life of Christ (For Youth).* Bruce Publ. Co., 1960. (Good for use with elementary level through Junior High.)

"HOW-TO" GUIDES FOR SHARED PRAYER AND SCRIPTURE PRAYER

Caprio, Betsy. *Experiments In Prayer.* Ave Maria Press, 1973.

———. *Experiments in Growth.* Ave Maria Press, 1976.

Huelsman, Richard, S.J. *Pray—An Introduction to the Spiritual Life for Busy People.* Paulist Press, 1976. (Moderator's manual also available.)

Link, Mark, S.J. *You—Prayer for Beginners and Those Who Have Forgotten How.* Argus Communications, 1976. (Contains suggestions for group shared prayer and praying with Scripture.)

Read and Pray Series: Franciscan Herald Press, 1974–1976.
Perkins, Pheme. *Gospel of St. John.*
Senior, Donald, C.P. *Gospel of St. Matthew.*
VanLinden, Philip. *Gospel of St. Mark.*
Karris, Robert. *Gospel of St. Luke.*

APPENDIX B
PUBLISHERS AND DISTRIBUTORS FOR YOUTH MINISTRY RESOURCE MATERIALS

Alba House Communications
Canfield, Ohio 44406

Alpha-Omega Prod.
821 So. Glendale Blvd.
Glendale, Calif. 91205

Argus Communications
Mr. Jack Gargiulo
7440 Natchez Ave.
Niles, Illinois 60648
(312-647-7800)

Benziger (Division of Bruce & Glencoe)
Mr. Dennis Ryan
17337 Ventura Blvd.
Encino, Calif. 91316
(213-894-1055)

William C. Brown and Co.
2460 Kerper Blvd.
Dubuque, Iowa 52001

Franciscan Communication Center
1229 South Santee St.
Los Angeles, Calif. 90015
(213-748-8331)

Genesis Project
145 West 58 St.
New York, N.Y. 10019
(800-223-9922)

Paulist Press
545 Island Rd.
Ramsey, N.J. 07446

William H. Sadlier Inc.
11 Park Place
New York, N.Y. 10007

St. Anthony Messenger Press
1615 Republic Street
Cincinnato, Ohio 45210
(513-241-5615)

St. Mary's College Press
Winona, Minnesota 55987

Serendipity House
Box 461
Scottdale, Pa. 15683

Silver Burdett
250 James St.
Morristown, New Jersey 07960

Twenty-Third Publications
Box 180
West Mystic, Connecticut 06388

Winston Press
25 Groveland Terrace
Minneapolis, Minn. 55403

Chapter 6
SCRIPTURE STUDY AND PRAYER RESOURCES

RESOURCES RECOMMENDED BOOKS FOR SCRIPTURE STUDY AND PRAYER

Some "Tools" For Gospel Study

New American Bible. Catholic Book Publishing Co.

The Jerusalem Bible. Doubleday & Co.

Divio-Afflante Spiritu. National Catholic Welfare Conference Publications, 1943. (Encyclical by Pope Pius XII promoting Biblical studies.)

Divine Revelation—Vatican II Documents. Guild, American & Association Press, 1966. (Modern methods of interpretation of Scripture.)

Evangelization in the Modern World. U.S. Catholic Conference Publications Office, 1975. (Pope Paul VI's Encyclical on methods of proclaiming the "Good News" today.)

Hartdegen, S. *Complete Verbal Concordance to the New American Bible.* Thomas Nelson, 1977.

Young, Robert *Analytical Concordance to the Bible.* Wm. B. Erdmans Co.

New World Dictionary Concordance—Use with NAB. Collins-World.

MacKenzie, S.J., John. *Dictionary of the Bible.* Bruce Publishers, 1965.

Nave, Orville J. *Nave's Topical Bible.* Guardian Press, 1975.

Martin, George. *Reading Scripture as the Word of God.* Word of Life, 1975. (Practical approaches and attitudes in reading, studying and praying Scripture.)

Harrington, Wilfrid. *The New Guide to Reading and Studying the Bible.* Michael Glazier, Inc., 1978.

Dalpadado, O.M.I., J. Kingsley. *Reading the Bible—A Guide to the Word of God for Everyone.* St. Paul Editions, 1973.

The Bible and You. Channing L. Bete Co., 1971. (A Scriptographic booklet.)

Garvin, Mary. *Bible Study Can Be Exciting!* Zondervan Publishing House, 1976.

Coleman, Lyman. *Encyclopedia of Serendipity.* Serendipity House, 1976.

Great People of the Bible and How They Lived. The Reader's Digest Assoc., Pleasantville, New York, 1974.

Frank, Harry T. *Discovering the Biblical World.* Hammond Inc., 1975.

Terrien, Samuel. *The Golden Bible Atlas.* Western Publication Co., 1975.

Daniel-Rops, Henri, *Daily Life in the Time of Jesus.* Hawthorn Books, 1962.

Heyer, Robert (Editor). *Scripture and the Church.* Paulist Press, 1976.

Jones, Alexander. *Unless Some Man Show Me.* Paulist Press, 1978. (Probing the Bible's problems.)

OLD TESTAMENT AND NEW TESTAMENT COMMENTARIES AND DISCUSSION STUDY GUIDES

Brown, S.S., Raymond, Joseph Fitzmyer, S.J., and Roland Murphy, O.C.D., Editors, *Jerome Biblical Commentary.* Prentice-Hall, 1968.

Nelson's Catholic Biblical Commentary.

Winzen, O.S.B., Damasus. *Pathways in Scripture.* Word of Life, 1976. (A book-by-book guide to the spiritual riches of the Bible.)

Humitz, Robert. *Man Meets God.* Benziger, Inc., 1973. (Guide to great themes of Scripture.) Teacher's manual available.

Tickle, Rev. John. *Discovering the Bible.* Liguori Publ., 1978. (Simple keys for learning and praying.) Teacher's manual available.

Scripture Discussion Commentary. ACTA Foundation, Chicago, 1972. (12 volumes on Old and New Testament.)

Herald Biblical Booklet Series. Franciscan Herald Press, 1972. (Ten pamphlets on Old and New Testament themes.)

Old and New Testament Reading Guides. Liturgical Press, 1960. (30 Old Testament guides, 14 New Testament guides.)

Barclay, William. *The Daily Study Bible Series.* Westminster Press, 1975. (17 volumes on books of the New Testament)

McKenzie, S.J., John. *The Power and the Wisdom.* Bruce Publ. Co., 1965. (An interpretation of the New Testament.)

Link, S.J., Mark. *The Seventh Trumpet.* Argus Communications, 1978. (The Good News proclaimed.)

Ciuba, Rev. Edward. *Who Do You Say That I Am?* Alba House, 1974. (An adult inquiry into the first three Gospels.)

Throckmorton, Burton. (Editor) *Gospel Parallels.* Thomas Nelson, Inc., 1967. (A synopsis of the first three Gospels.)

Kirk, Rev. Albert and Rev. Robert Obach. *A Commentary on the Gospel of Matthew.* Paulist Press, 1978. (Includes guides for study-questions and passages for praying Scripture.)

McBride, O.Praem, Alfred. *The Kingdom and the Glory.* Arena Lettres, 1976. (Commentary and meditation on Gospel of Matthew.)

Senior, C.P., Donald. *Invitation to Matthew.* Image Books, 1977.

O'Connor, Daniel and Jacques Jimenez. *The Images of Jesus: Exploring the Metaphors in Matthew's Gospel.* Winston Press, 1977.

Achtemeier, Paul J. *Invitation to Mark.* Image Books, 1978.

Smith, Thomas J. *Good News About Jesus as Told by Mark.* St. Mary's College Press, 1977. (Comes with a Guide for Group Leaders.)

———. *Jesus Alive! The Mighty Message of Mark.* St. Mary's College Press, 1975.

Karris, O.F.M., Robert. *Invitation to Luke.* Image Books, 1977.

Perkins, Pheme. *The Gospel of John.* Franciscan Herald Press, 1978.

MacRae, George W. *Invitation to John.* Image Books, 1978.

Wcela, Emil. *God's Word Today Series.* Pueblo Publishing Co., 1976. (8 volumes on Old and New Testament.)

Ellis, C.SS.R., Peter. *The Men and the Message of the Old Testament.* Liturgical Press, 1963.

Link, S.J., Mark. *These Stones Will Shout.* Argus Communications, 1975. (A new voice for the Old Testament.) Teacher's manual available.

McKenzie, S.J., John. *The Two-Edged Sword.* Image Books, 1956. (Interpretation of the Old Testament.)

Sheehan, S.J., John, F. X. *The Threshing Floor.* Paulist Press, 1973. (An interpretation of the Old Testament.)

———. *Let the People Cry Amen.* Paulist Press, 1978. (An inquiry into the oral history of the Old Testament.)

Murphy, O.Carm., Roland E., *The Psalms, Job* (Proclamation Commentary Series.) Fortress Press, Philadelphia, 1977.

Fischer, James. *The Psalms: I Will Be Their God and They Shall Be My People.* Alba Books, 1974.

Perkins, Pheme. *Reading the New Testament—An Introduction.* Paulist Press, 1978. (Readable, truly solid one-volume introduction to each book of the New Testament. Excellent for beginning Bible students, whether in top grades of high school, college or interested laity. For additional enrichment use with Paulist Press' cassette set *"Toward Understanding the New Testament"* and Service Evangelists Filmstrips Series.)

Harrington, O.P., Wilfrid J. *Explaining the Gospels.* Paulist Press, 1978.

Vawter, C.M., Bruce. *The Four Gospels.* Image Books, 1967. (An Introduction.)

ENRICHMENT BOOKS ON NEW TESTAMENT THEMES

Guardini, Rev. Ramano. *The Lord.* Henry Regnery Co., 1954.

Sheen, Archbishop Fulton J. *Life of Christ.* McGraw-Hill Book Co., 1958.

The Gospel of Jesus. Edizioni Instituto S. Gaetano, 1969.

O'Grady, John F. *Jesus, Lord and Christ.* Paulist Press, 1973. (The meaning of the New Testament Jesus.)

Santucci, Luigi. *Meeting Jesus—A New Way to Christ.* Herder & Herder, 1971.

Sertillanges, A. D. *Jesus.* Dimension Books, 1976.

Maloney, S.J., George. *Bright Darkness—Jesus Christ.* Dimension Books, 1976.

———. *Nesting in the Rock—Jesus the Way to the Father.* Dimension Books, 1977.

Cormier, Henri. *The Humor of Jesus.* Alba House, 1977.

Harrington, Wilfrid. *Parables Told by Jesus: A Contemporary Approach to the Parables.* Alba House, 1974.

———. *A Key to the Parables.* Paulist Press, 1978.

Flood, Rev. Edmund. *Parables of Jesus.* Paulist Press, 1978.

Richards, H. J. *The Miracles of Jesus—What Really Happened?* Fontana Books, 1975.

Martin, George. *Healing—Reflections on the Gospel.* Servant Books, 1977.

MacNutt, O.P., Francis. *Healing.* Ave Maria Press, 1974.

Fulco, S.J., William. *Maranatha.* Paulist Press, 1975. (Reflections on the mystical theology of John the Evangelist.)

McBride, O.Praem, Alfred. *The Gospel of the Holy Spirit.* Arena Lettres, 1975. (Commentary on the Acts.)

Smith, Thomas J. *Alive in the Spirit.* St. Mary's College Press, 1976. (The Church in the Acts of the Apostles.)

Acts of the Apostles. Edizioni Instituto Gaetano, 1972. (The early Church and its writings.)

Montague, S.M., George T. *The Holy Spirit.* Paulist Press, 1976. (Growth of a Biblical Tradition.)

Blenkinsopp, Joseph. *Jesus Is Lord—Paul's Life in Christ.* Paulist Press, 1964.

Montague, S.M., George T. *Building Christ's Body.* Franciscan Herald Press, 1975. (The dynamics for Christian living according to St. Paul.)

Grassi, Joseph. *The Secret of Paul the Apostle.* Orbis Books, 1978.

Maloney, S.J., George. *Mary—The Womb of God.* Dimension Books, 1976.

Mussner, Franz. *What Did Jesus Teach About the End of the World?* Word of Life, 1975.

Randall, S.T.D., John. *The Book of Revelation, What Does It Really Say?* Living Flame Press, 1976.

ENRICHMENT BOOKS FOR PRAYING SCRIPTURE AND BIBLICAL SPIRITUALITY

Martin, George. *Reading Scripture As the Word of God.* Word of Life, 1975. (Practical approaches and attitudes.)

Rosage, S.J., Msgr. David. *Discovering Pathways to Prayer.* Living Flame Press, 1977.

Huelsman, S.J., Richard J. *Pray—An Introduction to the Spiritual Life for Busy People.* Paulist Press, 1976. (Includes suggestions for praying Scripture.) Moderator's manual available.

Link, S.J., Mark. *You—Prayer for Beginners and Those Who Have Forgotten How.* Argus Communications, 1976.

LaVerdiere, S.S.S., Eugene, *Trumpets of Beaten Metal.* Liturgical Press, 1974. (Biblical Prayer).

Lussier, S.S.S., Ernest. *Biblical Prayer.* Liturgical Press, 1977.

Kosicki, S.S.B., George W. *The Key to the Good News—Jesus Christ Is Lord!* Dove Publ., 1975.

Van Kaam, C.S.Sp., Adrian. *Woman At the Well—Formative Scripture Reading.* Dimension Books, 1976.

———. *Looking for Jesus—Prayerful Presence to Scripture.* Dimension Books, 1977.

Loew, Rev. Jacques. *Face to Face with God—The Bible's Way to Pray.* Paulist Press, 1977.

Hocken, Peter. *Prayer—A Gift of Life.* Paulist Press, 1974. (Chapter: *Responding to God's Word*.)

Sheets, S.J., John. *The Spirit Speaks in Us—Biblical Way of Praying.* Dimension Books, 1968.

Stuhlmueller, C.P., Carroll. *Thirsting for the Lord—Essays in Biblical Spirituality.* Alba House, 1977.

Haughey, S.J., John C. *The Conspiracy of God: The Holy Spirit In Us.* Image Books, 1976.

Suenens, Cardinal Leon J. *A New Pentecost?* Seabury Press, 1975.

Schnackenburg, Rudolf. *Belief in the New Testament.* Paulist Press, 1978. (Contemplative essays of a believer.)

Fischer, C.M., John. *The Psalms: I Will Be Their God and They Shall Be My People.* Alba Books, 1974.

Stradling, Leslie. *Praying the Psalms.* Fortress Press, 1977.

Gelin, P.S.S., Albert. *The Psalms Are Our Prayers.* Liturgical Press, 1961.

Walls, Ronald. *The Glory of Israel.* Our Sunday Visitor, Inc., 1972. (Scriptural background on the mysteries of the rosary.)

Scriptural Rosary. Scriptural Rosary Center, Six N. Michigan Ave., Chicago, Illinois 60602. (A modern version of the way the rosary was once prayed throughout Western Europe in the late Middle Ages.)

Rosage, S.J., Msgr. David. *Speak Lord, Your Servant Is Listening.* Living Flame Press, 1976.

———. *Praying with Scripture in the Holy Land.* Living Flame Press, 1977. (Daily meditations with the Risen Jesus.)

Stuhlmueller, C.P., Carroll. *Biblical Meditations for Lent.* Paulist Press, 1978.

Read and Pray Series. Franciscan Herald Press, 1974. (Four pamphlets, one on each Gospel.)

Scripture for Meditation Series. Alba House, 1975. (Eleven booklets each developing a theme of Scripture.)

Barclay, William. *The Daily Study Bible Series.* Westminster Press, 1975. (17 volumes on books of the New Testament.)

Link, S.J., Mark. *The Mustard Seed.* Argus Communications, 1973. (A prayer guide to Mark's Gospel.)

Bloom, Archbishop Anthony, *Meditations—A Spiritual Journey Through the Parables.* Dimension Books, 1971.

Kersten, S.V.D., John C., *Bible Meditations for Every Day.* Catholic Book Publ. Co., 1978.

de la Croix, O.C.D., Paul-Marie, *The Biblical Spirituality of St. John.* Alba House, 1966.

Maloney, S.J., George, *Listen Prophets! An Urgent Call to Every Christian.* Dimension Books, 1972.

SUNDAY LITURGICAL READING GUIDES

Gaffney, James, *Biblical Notes for the Sunday Lectionary.* Paulist Press, 1978.

Scripture in Church. Subscriptions from Costello Publications, Inc., P.O. Box 9, Northport, L.I., New York, 11768. (Booklet published quarterly in collaboration with the U.S. Center for the Catholic Biblical Apostolate and the Irish Biblical Assoc. Commentary and homiletic aids for Sunday liturgical readings. One year subscription—$18.95.)

Discover the Bible. Bible Centre of Montreal, 2000 Sherbrooke St. West, Montreal, Quebec, Canada H3H1G4. (Weekly leaflet which comments on the Sunday readings. One year subscription—$8.50.)

Michael, Rev. Peter. *Traveling Along the Gospel Trail.* (Three volumes: Matthew, Cycle I; Mark, Cycle II; and Luke, Cycle III.) Arnoldus Press, Inc., 1916 Oroquieta, Sta. Cruz, Manila.

RECOMMENDED TAPED TALKS FOR SCRIPTURE PROGRAMS

Many of these taped talks have been used beneficially in established home or parish Scripture Programs. We advise leaders of home or parish programs to personally preview all taped talks and evaluate them for the interest and needs of their individual groups. Additional tapes are listed in catalogues from distributors and publishers.

SCRIPTURE PROGRAM EXPLANATION

Meeting Christ in Scripture Programs (2 cassette set), by Roger and Dianne Miller. So. Calif. Renewal Center, 1978. (Part I—explanation of Scripture Program format and purpose. Part II—how to begin a home or parish Scripture Program.)

PRAYING SCRIPTURE EXPLANATION

Brotherhood: A New Way of Living—Praying Scripture (1 cassette), by Msgr. David Rosage, S.J. So. Calif. Renewal Center, 1974. (Used to introduce praying Scripture in early meetings of each program year.)

Praying and Living with Scriptures (1 cassette), by Rev. Ralph Tichenor, S.J. So. Calif. Renewal Center, 1976.

Praying with the Scriptures (1 cassette), by Rev. Eugene La Verdiere S.S.S. National Catholic Reporter Cassettes, 1977.

Biblical Prayer (1 cassette), by Rev. James Walsh. National Catholic Reporter Cassettes, 1977.

Praying the Psalms (1 cassette), by Rev. Thomas Dubay, S.M. Alba House Communications, 1977.

INTRODUCTORY OVERVIEW OF OLD AND NEW TESTAMENTS

Great Themes of Scripture—Overview of the Old Testament (6 cassettes, 6 talks each 60 minutes in length), by Rev. Richard Rohr, O.F.M. St. Anthony Messenger Tapes, 1973. Titles in series are:
The Call: Introduction to the Word,
Exodus: The Journey of Faith,
Joshua to Kings: Ordinary Becomes Extraordinary,
The Prophets: Radical Traditionalists,
Genesis: God and Man, Job: Good and Evil,
Salvation History: Faith in Evolution.

Great Themes of Scripture—Overview of the New Testament (6 cassettes, 6 talks each 60 minutes in length), by Rev. Richard Rohr O.F.M. St. Anthony Messenger Tapes, 1973.

Jesus and His Church—Overview of the New Testament (6 cassettes, 6 talks each 60 minutes in length), by Rev. Richard Rohr, O.F.M. So. Calif. Renewal Center, 1976. (Up-dated presentation of 1973 series, used in introductory first-year programs following Fr. Rohr's "Overview of the Old Testament" series.) Titles in series are:
Matthew's Good News: The Reign of God,
Mark and John: Jesus is Lord,
Luke and Acts: A New Life,
Mary, Prayer and the Church,
Paul: A Life in Christ,
Apocalypse: The New Creation.

Enjoying the Old Testament (3 cassettes, 6 talks each 30 minutes in length), by Rev. George Montague S.M. Argus Communications, 1976. Includes study guides.

Enjoying the New Testament (3 cassettes, 6 talks each 30 minutes in length), by Rev. George Montague S.M. Argus Communications, 1976. Includes study guides.

Towards Understanding the New Testament (9 cassettes, 18 talks each 20 minutes in length), edited by Rev. Lawrence Boadt, C.S.P. Paulist Press, 1978. Includes study guides with outlines and discussion questions. (Provides indepth overview of New Testament. Study guide offers thought-provoking questions that encourage group discussion and faith-sharing of Scriptures. Pheme Perkins' book "Reading the New Testament" complements the above tapes.) Titles and contributors are:
God's Revelation in the Bible, by Rev. James Reese, O.S.F.S.
What is Biblical "Inspiration"? by Rev. James Reese, O.S.F.S.

The Early Christian Community in Acts 1–9, by Rev. James Reese, O.S.F.S.
The Nature of "Gospel", by Rev. Eugene A. LaVerdiere, S.S.S.
The Gospel of Mark, by Rev. Eugene A. LaVerdiere, S.S.S.
The Gospels of Matthew and Luke, by Rev. Eugene A. LaVerdiere, S.S.S.
St. Paul's Life and Ministry in Acts 12–28, by Rev. Terence J. Keegan, O.P.
St. Paul's First Letter to the Corinthians, by Rev. Terence J. Keegan, O.P.
St. Paul's Epistles to the Galatians and the Romans, by Rev. Terence J. Keegan, O.P.
The Epistle to the Philippians, by Rev. James Turro
The Epistles to the Colossians and Ephesians, by Rev. James Turro
The Pastoral Epistles to Timothy and Titus, by Rev. James Turro
The First Epistle to St. Peter, by Rev. Anthony Tambasco, S.M.M.
The Epistle of St. James, by Rev. Anthony Tambasco, S.M.M.
The Gospel of John, Part I, by Rev. Richard Dillon
The Gospel of John, Part II and the Johannine Letters, by Rev. Richard Dillon
The Epistle to the Hebrews, by Msgr. Myles M. Bourke
The Book of Revelation (Apocalypse), by Rev. Lawrence Boadt, C.S.P.

OLD TESTAMENT THEMES

Exodus—Genesis (9 cassettes, 9 talks each 60 minutes in length), by Rev. Frank Montalbano. Christian Media, 1978. (Presented at Charismatic Biblical Institute, San Antonio, Texas, 1978.)

The Psalms (10 cassettes, 10 talks each 60 minutes in length), by Rev. George Montague, S.M. Christian Media, 1978. (Presented at Charismatic Biblical Institute, 1978, San Antonio, Texas.)

The Psalms: A School of Prayer (6 cassettes, 6 talks each 45 minutes in length), by Rev. Roland E. Murphy, O.C.D. National Catholic Reporter Cassettes, 1976. Includes study guides.

Old Testament Prophecy (10 cassettes, 10 talks each 60 minutes in length), by Rev. George Montague, S.M. Order from Harold Harfoot. (Presented at Charismatic Biblical Institute, 1977.)

The Prophets: Charismatic Men (6 cassettes, 6 talks each 45 minutes in length), by Rev. Carroll Stuhlmueller, C.P. Argus Communications, 1977. Includes study guides.

Prophet Isaiah (7 cassettes, 7 talks each 45 minutes in length), by Rev. James Wolfe, O.S.B. Dove Publications, 1966.

Intercession—Old Testament Biblical Perspective (1 cassette, 60 minutes in length), by Rev. Patrick Crowley SS.CC. So. Calif. Renewal Center, 1976.

NEW TESTAMENT THEMES

Understanding the Gospels (5 cassettes, 5 talks each 60 minutes in length), by Rev. George Montague, S.M. Order from Harold Harfoot. (Presented at Charismatic Biblical Institute, 1977.)

The Gospel of Mark (10 cassettes, 20 talks each 20 minutes in length), by Rev. Donald Senior, C.P. National Catholic Reporter Cassettes, 1977. Includes study guides. (Interesting and easy to follow indepth study of Mark's Gospel.)

The Gospel of Mark (22 cassettes, 22 talks each 60 minutes in length), by Rev. James O'Bryne, S.T. Holy Spirit Cenacle Center, 1978. Includes study guides.

The Gospel of Mark (10 cassettes, 10 talks each 60 minutes in length), by Rev. Richard Rohr O.F.M. Order from Harold Harfoot. (Presented at Charismatic Biblical Institute, 1977.)

The Gospel of Mark (5 cassettes, 5 talks each 60 minutes in length), by Joseph Grassi, Catholic Biblical Professor and Scholar. Alba House Cassettes, 1977. (Vol. I of *"The Spiritual Message of the Gospels"* series. Series' emphasis is on revealing the spiritual insights in the Gospels with special attention given to the unique personal life-style of Jesus and the early Christians in the four Gospels.) Includes study guides.

The Gospel of Matthew (4 cassettes, 4 talks each 60 minutes in length), by Joseph Grassi, Catholic Biblical Professor and Scholar. Alba House Cassettes, 1977. Includes study guides. (Vol. II of "The Spiritual Message of the Gospels" series.)

Gospel of Matthew (5 cassettes, 5 talks each 60 minutes in length), by Rev. George Montague, S.M. Order from Harold Harfoot. (Presented at Charismatic Biblical Institute, 1977.)

The Gospel of Luke (10 cassettes, 10 talks each 60 minutes in length), by Rev. Richard Rohr O.F.M. Christian Media, 1978. (Presented at Charismatic Biblical Institute, 1978.)

The Gospel of Luke (4 cassettes, 4 talks each 60 minutes in length), by Joseph Grassi, Catholic Biblical Professor and Scholar. Alba House Cassettes, 1977. Includes study guides. (Vol. III of "The Spiritual Message of the Gospels" series.)

The Gospel of John (20 cassettes, 20 talks each 60 minutes in length), by Rev. James O'Bryne, S.T. Holy Spirit Cenacle Center, 1977. Includes study guides.

The Gospel of John (10 cassettes, 10 talks each 60 minutes in length), by Rev. Richard Rohr, O.F.M. Order from Harold Harfoot. (Presented at Charismatic Biblical Institute, 1977.)

The Gospel of John (5 cassettes, 5 talks each 60 minutes in length), by Joseph Grassi, Catholic Biblical Professor and Scholar. Alba House Cassettes, 1977. Includes study guides. (Vol. IV of "The Spiritual Message of the Gospels" series.)

The Gospel of St. John (12 cassettes, 24 talks each 20 minutes in length), by Rev. Stephen Doyle. National Catholic Reporter Cassette, 1977. Includes study guides.

Suffering to Glory: Passion Narratives and Resurrection Appearances (2 cassettes, 2 talks each 90 minutes in length), by Rev. Eugene LaVerdiere, S.S.S. National Catholic Reporter Cassettes, 1977.

Acts of the Apostles (5 cassettes, 5 talks each 60 minutes in length), by Rev. Frank Montalbano, O.M.I. Order from Harold Harfoot. (Presented at Charismatic Biblical Institute, 1977.)

Acts of the Apostles (9 cassettes, 9 talks each 60 minutes in length), by Rev. Richard Rohr, O.F.M. Christian Media, 1978. (Presented at Charismatic Biblical Institute, San Antonio, Texas.)

Paul: The Proclaimer (5 cassettes, 5 talks each 45 minutes in length), by Rev. Eugene LaVerdiere, S.S.S. National Catholic Reporter Cassettes, 1977. Includes study guides.

Themes in Paul (5 cassettes, 5 talks each 60 minutes in length), by Rev. Robert Sargent, S.M. Order from Harold Harfoot. (Presented at Charismatic Biblical Institute, 1977.)

Life and Journeys of St. Paul (3 cassettes, 3 talks each 90 minutes), by Rev. James O'Bryne, S.T., Holy Spirit Cenacle Center, 1975.

Epistle to the Galatians (7 cassettes, 7 talks each 90 minutes), by Rev. James O'Bryne, S.T., Holy Spirit Cenacle Center, 1975. (This set is a continuation of the series "Life and Journeys of St. Paul.")

Epistle to First Corinthians (9 cassettes, 9 talks each 90 minutes), by Rev. James O'Bryne, S.T., Holy Spirit Cenacle Center, 1976.

Epistle to Second Corinthians (10 cassettes, 10 talks each 90 minutes), by Rev. James O'Bryne, S.T., Holy Spirit Cenacle Center, 1976.

Ephesians (7 cassettes, 7 talks each 50 minutes) by Rev. James Wolfe, O.S.B., Dove Publications, 1976.

Corinthians (10 cassettes, 10 talks each 60 minutes in length), by Rev. George Montague, S.M. Christian Media, 1978. (Presented at Charismatic Biblical Institute, 1978.)

Colossians/Ephesians (10 cassettes, 10 talks each 60 minutes in length), by Rev. Robert Sargent, S.M. Christian Media, 1978. (Presented at Charismatic Biblical Institute, 1978.)

Revelations (6 cassettes, 6 talks each 50 minutes in length), by Rev. James Wolfe, O.S.B. Dove Publications, 1978.

Book of Revelation (10 cassettes, 10 talks each 60 minutes in length), by Rev. Frank Montalbano, O.M.I. Order from Harold Harfoot. (Presented at Charismatic Biblical Institute, 1977.)

The Book of Revelation (8 cassettes, 16 talks each 20 minutes in length), by Rev. Stephen Doyle. National Catholic Reporter Cassettes, 1978. Includes study guides.

SINGLE TALKS ON NEW TESTAMENT THEMES

Jesus Christ: Model Intercessor (1 cassette), by Rev. Ralph Tichenor, S.J. So. Calif. Renewal Center, 1976.

Christ's Healing Ministry in the Gospels (1 cassette), by Rev. Patrick Crowley, SS.CC. Charis Tapes, 1976.

Christian Living and the Beatitudes (1 cassette), by Rev. Patrick Crowley, SS.CC. Charis tapes, 1976.

Mary Revealed Through Scripture (1 cassette), by Rev. James O'Bryne, S.T., Holy Spirit Cenacle Center, 1978.

Los Angeles Religious Education Congress Scripture Presentations (1 cassette each), by leading Scripture scholars, available from Tapette Corp. Talks include:

The Gospel Preached, Sweet Candy or Bitter Pill by Rev. Emery Tang, O.F.M., 1976.

The Psalms: Israel's Prayers by Rev. Roland Murphy, O.Carm., 1978.

"Do This in Remembrance of Me" by Rev. Eugene LaVerdiere, S.S.S., 1978.

Koinonia: Life in the Early Christian Community by Rev. Eugene LaVerdiere, S.S.S., 1978.

Paul: A Christian Odyssey by Rev. Eugene LaVerdiere, S.S.S., 1977.

Mark: Following the Suffering Messiah by Rev. Eugene LaVerdiere, S.S.S., 1977.

The Way to Emmaus—Luke 24:13–35 by Rev. Eugene LaVerdiere, S.S.S., 1977.

Free to Witness and *Scripture Is Credible/Professional Dynamic*, both by Rev. Mark Link, S.J., 1976. (Both have concrete suggestions for dynamic approaches to teaching Scripture.)

CASSETTES—BIBLICAL MEDITATIONS WITH MUSIC

Suggested for use in the **PRAYING SCRIPTURE phase** of program meetings.

Savary, S.J., L. *Meditations with Music—C Cycle* (Liturgical Year), 7 tapes.

———, *Biblical Meditations—I* (A Miracle Story, A Parable), 1 tape.

———, *Biblical Meditations—II* (A Life-event, A Prayer-psalm), 1 tape.

———, *Psalms of Reconciliation* (Psalms of Forgiveness and Hope), 1 tape.

All above are available from National Catholic Reporter Cassettes.

RECORDED SONGS BASED ON SCRIPTURE PASSAGES

The following recorded albums are comprised of many songs based on Scripture. Some albums are available on cassette.

Landry, Rev. C. *Abba, Father—Prayer Songs*. North American Liturgy Resources (NALR).

Conry, T. *Ashes*. NALR.

Foley, S.M., J. *Wood Hath Hope.* NALR.

The Dameans. *Remember Your Love.* NALR.

St. Louis Jesuits. *Earthen Vessels.* NALR.

———, *A Dwelling Place.* NALR.

———, *Neither Silver nor Gold.* NALR.

Monks of Western Priory. *Wherever You Go.* Western Priory Productions, Inc.

———, *Locusts and Wild Honey.* Western Priory Productions, Inc.

———, *Listen.* Western Priory Productions, Inc.

———, *Calm Is the Night.* Western Priory Productions, Inc.

———, *Spirit Alive.* Western Priory Productions, Inc.

Men's Pontifical Choir of St. Joseph, Kansas City. *Familiar Gregorian Chant.* National Catholic Reporter Cassettes.

Meditations on the Psalms. Mark IV Productions.

And Jesus Said. Mark IV Productions.

TAPE, BOOK AND RECORD DISTRIBUTORS

Religious Lending Tape Libraries

Private and public tape lending libraries are developing throughout the country. We suggest looking for them in your area by checking through the local diocesan adult religious education office, local Catholic high schools and colleges, hospitals, parish religious education programs, and prayer meeting tape ministries. Usually such lending tape libraries have catalogues available upon request and charge a minimal fee for use of their services. These libraries provide a means of previewing Scripture tapes and records before deciding to purchase them for home or parish Scripture Program use. Small home groups will especially benefit from this service when available.

Publishers and Distributors

Most resources for Scripture study and prayer are available for purchase through local religious book stores. They can also be ordered direct from the following publishers and distributors. Their catalogues are available upon request.

ALBA HOUSE CASSETTES AND BOOKS
Canfield, Ohio 44406

ARGUS COMMUNICATIONS
3505 N. Ashland Ave.
Chicago, Illinois 60657

CHARISMATIC RENEWAL SERVICES
P.O. Box 617
Ann Arbor, Michigan 48107

CHARIS TAPES (Spanish)
P.O. Box 506
La Puente, California 91747
213-968-9595

CHRISTIAN MEDIA
P.O. Box 748
Ogden, Utah 84402
312-485-3925

DOVE PUBLICATIONS
Pecos, New Mexico 87552
505-757-6597

HAROLD HARFOOT
4430 South West 34th Drive
Ft. Lauderdale, Florida 33312
305-983-8193
(Only for 1977 Charismatic Biblical Institute Tapes.)

HOLY SPIRIT CENACLE CENTER
525 E. Maple Ave.
Orange, California 92666
714-633-2652

LITURGICAL PRESS
Collegeville, Minnesota 56321

MARK IV PRODUCTIONS
P.O. Box 128
Arnandville, Louisiana 70512

NATIONAL CATHOLIC REPORTER (NCR) CASSETTES
Dept. CC, P.O. Box 281
Kansas City, Missouri 64141

NORTH AMERICAN LITURGY RESOURCES
2110 West Peoria Avenue
Phoenix, Arizona 85029
602-943-7229

PAULIST PRESS
545 Island Rd.
Ramsey, N.J. 07446
201-825-7300

ST. ANTHONY MESSENGER PRESS
1615 Republic Street
Cincinnati, Ohio 45210
513-241-5615

SERENDIPITY HOUSE
Box 461
Scottdale, Pa. 15683

SOUTHERN CALIFORNIA RENEWAL CENTER (SCRC)
5730 Manchester Blvd.
Los Angeles, California 90045
213-645-1162

TAPETTE CORP.
7221 Garden Grove Blvd.
Garden Grove, California 92641
714-638-7960
(L.A. Religious Education Congress Talks)

THOMAS MORE CASSETTES
180 W. Wabash Avenue
Chicago, Illinois 60601

WESTERN PRIORY PRODUCTIONS, INC.
Weston, Vermont 05161

AUDIO-VISUAL MEDIA FOR SCRIPTURE STUDY AND PRAYER

VIDEO TAPES FOR SCRIPTURE STUDY

Video Tapes (Color, 45 to 60 min., ½ inch Beta-2 or VHS) are available from Christian Media. These Bible teachings were video taped at the Charismatic Biblical Sessions Institute in San Antonio, Texas, 1978 and 1979. A sample video-tape lecture from the below listed series is available for a fee.

"Genesis, Exodus" (9 lectures) by Rev. Frank Montalbano, O.M.I. Beginning in faith and covenant and the relevance of these great themes for Christian living today.

"Psalms" (10 lectures) by Rev. George Montague, S.M. How the Spirit-inspired songs of Israel are inspired prayers for us today.

"Luke" (10 lectures) by Rev. Richard Rohr, O.F.M.
"Acts" (9 lectures) by Rev. Richard Rohr, O.F.M. How the Spirit-full Jesus and his Spirit-filled community first lived the "Good News" and brought it to the world.

"Corinthians" (10 lectures) by Rev. George Montague, S.M. How Paul preached to and taught his charismatic communities. God's plan of salvation in Christ Jesus and the role of the Holy Spirit in the Christian journey.

"Colossians, Ephesians" (10 lectures) by Rev. Robert Sargent, S.M. The headship of Christ and God's plan of salvation in the mystery of the Church, according to Paul's blueprint.

FILMS AND FILMSTRIPS SCRIPTURE STUDY

"New Media Bible" (Color, 20 min., 16mm films, each with additional 35mm filmstrip and cassettes and explanatory "Bible Times" magazine) available from *The Genesis Project*. First ten films cover Genesis 1–22 (Creation to Abraham's Sacrifice of Isaac) and Luke 1–2 (the Annunciation, Nativity and Jesus' youth). Open-ended project, additional films released periodically until entire Bible is covered.

"Literary Forms: A Key to Understand the Bible" (Color, 20 min., filmstrip with cassette), available from ACTA Foundation. Explanation of types of literary form in a Scripture passage to enable the reader to distinguish what the passage means rather than what its words literally say.

"Jerusalem, 66 A.D." (Color, 42 min., filmstrip with cassette), available from ACTA Foundation. A view of the Jerusalem of Christ's time as revealed by examination of a scale model of the city in 66 A.D., historical writings and modern archeological digs.

"Exodus of Israel" (Color, 20 min., 35mm filmstrip with record), available from Alpha-Omega Productions. Unfolds events from Book of Exodus which the Church links with the Mass. (Part I of *Understanding the Liturgy Series*.)

*"The Exodus" (Color, 28 min., 16mm film), available from Mass Media Ministries. An account of God's chosen people's desert experience with a visual portrayal of the birthplace of the Judaeo-Christian traditions.

*"Where Jesus Lived" (Family Films, Color, 14 min., 16mm film), available from Roa Films. The places of Jesus' life, death and resurrection with references to the lifestyle of Jesus' time.

*"The Passover" (Gospel Films, Color, 30 min., 16mm film, available from Roa Films.) An introduction to the Jewish feast in which the Christian Eucharist is rooted.

*"Nomad Life of the Hebrews" and "Religious Life of the Hebrews" in *Old Testament Life and Times* (K-28), Alba House (35mm filmstrip with record).

*"The Geography of the Holy Land," (K-28), Alba House (35mm filmstrip with record).

*"Archaeology and the Living New Testament" (Film Services, Color, 25 min., 16mm film), available from Roa Films. The setting of the last week of Jesus' ministry and the work of his first followers.

*"The Gospel According to St. Matthew" (136 min., Black and White, 16mm film), available from Audio Brandon Films. A simple but profound presentation of Matthew's account of the life of Jesus.

*"The Gospel According to Matthew," *The Four Gospels* (K-98), Alba House (35mm filmstrip with record).

*Boadt, Rev. Lawrence, C.S.P. "Matthew—Discipleship." *Service Evangelists Filmstrip Series*, Paulist Press (35mm filmstrip with record or cassette). An examination of the nature of true discipleship seen in the Sermon on the Mount.

*"Sermon on the Mount, Now" (19 min., Color, 16mm film), available from Mass Media Ministries. A reading of the Sermon on the Mount with modern images that highlight the ethics of Christ.

*"The Gospel According to Mark," *The Four Gospels* (K-98) Alba House (35mm filmstrip with record).

*Keegan, Rev. Terence J., O.P. "Mark—Christian Kerygma," *Service Evangelists Filmstrip Series*, Paulist Press (35mm filmstrip with cassette or record). A portrayal of the events of Jesus' life as recounted in Mark's Gospel.

*Perkins, Pheme, Ph.D. "Luke—Prayer and Social Apostolate." *Service Evangelists Filmstrip Series*, Paulist Press (35mm filmstrip with cassette or record). The relationship of prayer and social action in Luke's portrayal of Jesus.

*"The Gospel According to Luke," *The Four Gospels* (K-98), Alba House (35mm filmstrip with record).

*Malatesta, Rev. Edward, S.J. "John—Spirituality and Sacrament." *Service Evangelists Filmstrip Series*, Paulist Press (35mm filmstrip with cassette or record). An understanding of Jesus' mission through a look at John's accounts of Jesus' personal interactions with others.

*"The Gospel According to John," *The Four Gospels* (K-98), Alba House (35mm filmstrip with record).

*"The Conversion" (Cathedral Films, 30 min., Black and White, 16mm film), available from Roa Films. The story of Paul's persecution of Christians and his subsequent conversion, based on Acts 9.

*"Many Different Gifts" (50 min., Color, 16mm film), available from Mass Media Ministries. Portrait of the celebrations of a non-territorial Catholic community.

*"The Parable" (22 min., Color, 16mm film), available from Mass Media Ministries. An award winning film that presents a Christian parable in contemporary terms.

"Song for the Universe" (Color, 35mm filmstrip with record), available from Paulist Press. The spirit of Genesis and Teilhard de Chardin mingle with the freshness of clear skies and unspoiled earth in this visual and poetic psalm. Good for praying Scripture. (Contemplation on the New Earth Series).

"Tower of Babel" (Color, 10 min., 16mm film), available from Franciscan Communication Center. An animated version of the Biblical tale.

"Psalm 23" (14 color slides with guide), available from Pflaum. Psalm 23, "The Lord Is My Shepherd," provides the central focus for these slides on prayer. The verses seem to sum up the life attitudes of the truly religious person. Good for Scripture prayer. (Witness Series)

"We Have Seen the Lord" (30 slides with script), available from Paulist Press. Visuals for "Come to the Father—Book 4." A visual pilgrimage to the Holy Land with emphasis on places of importance in the life of the Lord. Good aid for praying Scripture.

"Out of Darkness" (Color, 35mm filmstrip with record), available from Klise. A sensory experience with picture, word and music—all revealing God's love for us and our love in Christ, for one another. Good for praying Scripture.

"Come to Life" (Color, 11 min., 16mm film), a TeleKETIC film from Franciscan Communication Center. A film filled with a sense of wonder, life, growth and movement illustrating an everchanging world permeated with the presence of an unchanging God that proclaims the Gospel message of Salvation.

"Buttercup" (Color, 11 min., 16mm film), available from Franciscan Communication Center. A poetic, meditative film montage tracing the passage of a buttercup floating in a mountain stream until it reaches the city. A modern, open-ended parable that can have many interpretations and inspire many parallels.

"Let Us Pray Series" (six sets of 36–40 slides with multi-resource guides), available from Paulist Press. Each series is suitable for the community at celebration, also very adaptable for use in praying Scripture sessions. Individual series include:

(1) *Easter*—Palm Sunday, Easter, Faith, Friendship;

(2) *Pentecost*—Pentecost, Corpus Christi, Freedom, Hope;

(3) *Advent*—Coming of the Lord, Listening to the Word, Love, Incarnation;

(4) *Lent*—Ash Wednesday, Fasting and Almsgiving, Penance, Poverty and Abundance;

(5) *Christian Mission*—Thanksgiving, Christ the King, Christ the Clown;

(6) *Christmas*—Peace, New Life, The Holy Family, Epiphany.

"Encounter" (Color, 8 min., 16mm film), available from TeleSPOTS, Franciscan Communication Center. Theme of the need to give and receive love is presented in six mini-episodes with Scripture verses.

"Search" (Color, 8 min., 16mm film), available from TeleSPOTS, Franciscan Communication Center. Theme of seeing God's presence in the world is highlighted in six mini-episodes with Scripture verses.

"Witness" (Color, 8 min., 16mm film), available from TeleSPOTS, Franciscan Communication Center. Theme to live the Gospel message is dramatized in six mini-episodes with Scripture verses.

"Images 1:1—Word Game, Incarnation," (Color, 2 min., 16mm film), available from TeleSPOTS, Franciscan Communication Center. First of five films of TeleSPOTS, each developing a theme that can be applied to Scripture and Christian living. Good for praying Scripture. Titles in other Image Series include:

"Images 1:2—Masks of Man, Walk Like a Man,"

"Images 1:3—Sleepy World, the Kiss,"

"Images 1:4—Elderly Poor, Dominion,"

"Images 1:5—Do You Ever Talk to God?, Psalm (139) for a Surfer."

"Advent Liturgy" (Color, 35mm filmstrip with record), available from Klise. This electronic homily emphasizes faith in the Christ of the first Christmas, hope in the Christ of the Second Coming, and charity toward the Christ we meet daily in our neighbor. Good for praying Scripture. (Social Gospel Series).

*"The Great Mystique Shatterer" (5 min., 35mm filmstrip with record), available from TeleKETICS. Various artistic representations of Jesus are the backdrop as two women discuss their images of Jesus.

*"It's About this Carpenter" (13 min., Black and White, 16mm film), available from Roa Films. A modern parable about a carpenter who delivers a cross to a church and encounters many different responses on his journey.

*Perkins, Pheme, Ph.D. "Who Is Jesus?" *Family Parish Religious Education*, (Paulist Press, 35mm filmstrip with cassette), available from Paulist Press. An examination of the many images of Jesus found in the Synoptic Gospels.

The Beatitudes Series: Four TeleKETIC films from Franciscan Communication Center. Includes: *"They Shall See"* (Color, 5 min., 16mm film), available from Franciscan Communication Center or Alba House Communications. Relates to the "pure of heart," who see oneness and wholeness in all things. Meditative presentation.

"Those Who Mourn" (Color, 5 min., 16mm film), available from Franciscan Communication Center or Alba House Communications. Through the dramatization of a woman, about to have a child, struggling to find meaning in the death of her husband, the beatitude of "Blessed are they who mourn" comes alive!

*"Theirs Is the Kingdom" (Color, 5 min., 16mm film), available from Franciscan Communication Center or Alba House Communications. Two boys' experience of putting into practice their ideals leads one of them to a deeper understanding of the meaning of "Blessed are the poor in spirit."

*"Matthew 5:5" (Color, 5 min., 16mm film), available from Franciscan Communication Center. A powerful sequence of images that emphasize the beatitude, "Blessed are the meek."

*Reese, Rev. James, O.S.F.S. *"Reconciliation in the Gospel of Matthew." Family Parish Religious Education*, Paulist Press (35mm filmstrip with cassette). A look at Jesus' call to his followers to be peacemakers in the world.

*"The Cure of the Crippled Man" (Color, 35mm filmstrip with record) available from TeleKETICS. Follows scriptural text (in John 5:1–15) of the story of the crippled man at the Sheep Pool.

"Talent for Tony" (Color, 13 min., 16mm film), available from TeleKETICS, Franciscan Communication Center. A contemporary story of relationship between father and son directly parallels the biblical story of the talents.

"Gifts and Talents" (Color, 35mm filmstrip with record), available from TeleKETICS. Call of modern Christians based on the parable of the talents.

"The Parable of the Good Samaritan" (Color, 7 min., 35mm filmstrip with record or cassette), available from St. Anthony Messenger Press. Contemporary dramatization of age-old question—"Who is my neighbor?"

"The Parable of the Unforgiving Debtor" (Color, 5½ min., 35mm filmstrip with record or cassette), available from St. Anthony Messenger Press. Contemporary dramatization of Christ's teaching on forgiveness.

"Bread and Wine" (Color, 5 min., 16mm film), a TeleKETIC film from Franciscan Communication Center, also available from Alba House Communications. Develops themes of Eucharist and community praising God for his gifts of food and love. Especially effective because of the music—Mozart's Great Mass "Sanctus."

"Eucharist (Holy Communion" (Color, 10 min., 16mm film) a TeleKETIC film available from Franciscan Communication Center. Uses many images threaded together by the liturgy to convey the Christian's experience of life is "summed up" in the liturgy.

*Freyne, Sean, Ph.D. *"Faith in the Gospel of Mark" Family Parish Religious Education*, Paulist Press (35mm filmstrip with cassette). An examination of the responses to Jesus characterized by people in Mark's Gospel.

*"The Greatest Dinner Party" (35mm filmstrip with record or cassette), available from TeleKETICS. A retelling of the Lucan banquet parable that stresses our invitation to be part of God's Kingdom.

*Keegan, Rev. Terence J., O.P. *"Prayer of Jesus in the Gospel of Luke" Family Parish Religious Education*, Paulist Press (35mm filmstrip with cassette).

*Hellwig, Monika, Ph.D. *"Eucharist in John's Gospel" Family Parish Religious Education*, Paulist Press (35mm filmstrip with cassette). A look at what it means to say that Jesus is the Bread of Life.

"Pentecost" (Color, 35mm filmstrip with record), available from TeleKETICS. The Pentecost event narrated in a light-hearted narration of the story in Acts 2:1–21 that emphasizes the strengthening presence of the Holy Spirit. Good for scriptural prayer.

"Spirit" (20 slides with resource guides), available from Mark IV Presentations. Multi-usage collection of slides which aid the viewer to explore his/her personal experience of the Spirit.

*Rohr, Rev. Richard, O.F.M. *"Community in the Acts of the Apostles" Family Parish Religious Education*, Paulist Press (35mm filmstrip with cassette). How the early Church lived the Gospel message.

*"Works of Faith" (kino Films, 12 min., Color, 16mm film), available from Roa Films. How the early Christians differed from the dominant culture in daily living and business practices.

"That Kind of Love" (Color, 35mm filmstrip with record), available from TeleKETICS. A strikingly visual exploration of John's first letter and the simple but profound message that God is love and that we, in turn are love because of him. Good for praying Scripture.

*"Right Here, Right Now" (TeleKETICS Films, 15 min., Color, 16mm film), available from Roa Films. An "Average" man changes the lives of six troubled people, who continue to their new way of life after his death.

*Perkins, Pheme, *"Reading the New Testament—An Introduction"* Paulist Press, 1978, pages 319–325. Audio-visual media selected to correspond with each chapter of text.

AUDIO-VISUAL MEDIA DISTRIBUTORS

There is a wide variety of audio-visual media suitable for Scripture study and/or Scripture prayer. Much good material is available for rental through diocesan religious education offices, and diocesan high-school and college libraries. Contact those institutions and offices for their catalogues and rental arrangements. Many parishes' religious education offices have also developed audio-visual libraries and their material is usually available for use in parish-related adult education programs. Below are listed publishers and distributors of audio-visual media, some of whom also have rental arrangements. Their catalogues are available upon request.

Films, Filmstrips, Slide Sets

ACTA Foundation
4848 North Clark
Chicago, Illinois 60640

ALBA HOUSE COMMUNICATIONS
Canfield, Ohio 44406

ALPHA-OMEGA PRODUCTIONS
821 So. Glendale Blvd.
Glendale, California 91205

AUDIO BRANDON FILMS
34 MacQuesten Parkway So.
Mount Vernon, New York 10550
914-664-5051

3868 Piedmont Avenue
Oakland, California 94611
415-658-9890

1619 No. Cherokee
Los Angeles, California 90028
213-463-1131

2512 Program Drive
Dallas, Texas 75220
214-357-6494

8400 Brookfield Avenue
Brookfield, Illinois 60513
312-485-3925

GENESIS PROJECT
145 West 58 Street
New York, New York 10019
800-223-9922

MARK IV PRODUCTIONS
P.O. Box 128
Arnandville, Louisiana 70512

MASS MEDIA MINISTRIES
2116 N. Charles Street
Baltimore, Maryland 21218
301-727-3270

1720 Chouteau Avenue
St. Louis, Missouri 63103
314-436-0418

PAULIST PRESS
545 Island Road
Ramsey, New Jersey 07446
201-825-7300

ROA FILMS
1696 North Astor Street
Milwaukee, Wisconsin 53202
414-271-0861
800-558-9015

ST. ANTHONY MESSENGER PRESS
1615 Republic Street
Cincinnati, Ohio 45210
513-241-5615

TeleKETICS
FRANCISCAN COMMUNICATION CENTER
1229 South Santee Street
Los Angeles, California 90015
213-748-2191

TWENTY-THIRD PUBLICATIONS
P.O. Box 180
Fort Wayne, Indiana 46801
219-742-1248

Video Tapes

CHRISTIAN MEDIA
P.O. Box 748
Ogden, Utah 84402
801-399-4006